A TIME
TO BUILD

ALSO BY YUVAL LEVIN

The Fractured Republic:
Renewing America's Social Contract in the Age of Individualism

The Great Debate:
Edmund Burke, Thomas Paine, and the Birth of Right and Left

Imagining the Future:
Science and American Democracy

A TIME TO BUILD

FROM FAMILY AND COMMUNITY
TO CONGRESS AND THE CAMPUS,
HOW RECOMMITTING TO OUR INSTITUTIONS
CAN REVIVE THE AMERICAN DREAM

YUVAL LEVIN

BASIC BOOKS
New York

Basic Books
Hachette Book Group
1290 Avenue of the Americas, New York, NY 10104
www.basicbooks.com

Printed in the United States of America
First Edition: January 2020

Published by Basic Books, an imprint of Perseus Books, LLC, a subsidiary of Hachette Book Group, Inc. The Basic Books name and logo is a trademark of the Hachette Book Group.

The Hachette Speakers Bureau provides a wide range of authors for speaking events. To find out more, go to www.hachettespeakersbureau.com or call (866) 376-6591.

The publisher is not responsible for websites (or their content) that are not owned by the publisher.

Print book interior design by Linda Mark.

Library of Congress Cataloging-in-Publication Data
Names: Levin, Yuval, author.
Title: A time to build: from family and community to Congress and the
   campus, how recommitting to our institutions can revive the American
   dream / Yuval Levin.
Description: New York : Basic Books, 2020. | Includes bibliographical
   references and index.
Identifiers: LCCN 2019033089 | ISBN 9781541699274 (hardcover) |
   ISBN 9781541699281 (ebook)
Subjects: LCSH: United States—Social conditions—21st century. |
   Associations, institutions, etc.—United States. | Consensus
   (Social sciences)—History—21st century. | American Dream.
Classification: LCC HN59.2 .L494 2020 | DDC 306.0973--dc23
LC record available at https://lccn.loc.gov/2019033089
ISBNs: 978-1-5416-9927-4 (hardcover), 978-1-5416-9928-1 (ebook)

LSC-C

10 9 8 7 6 5 4 3 2 1

For Cecelia, with love

CONTENTS

INTRODUCTION

TWO DECADES AGO, AT THE TURN OF THE MILLENNIUM, MANY Americans had a sense that we were living at the dawn of a new age—a bright and forward-looking era marked by stable economic progress and crowned by technological breakthroughs that might both liberate and unify us. Our country had real problems, of course, and the day that was dawning would bring challenges of its own, but it seemed that something exciting was afoot.

By now, it has become unavoidably evident that our country has experienced the beginning of this new millennium less as a dawn than as a twilight age. This century has certainly seen its share of novel technologies and of political, cultural, and social innovations. But all of these have seemed somehow to strain us more than they enable us. In politics, economics, world affairs, culture, media, and many other arenas, we have tried to extend into a new era some of the arrangements devised to serve us well in the second half of the twentieth century, and have been left with the sense that they are overstretched—and therefore increasingly rigid and brittle. But we don't yet know what might replace them.

The term "twilight age" has a particular meaning given by Robert Nisbet, one of the foremost American sociologists of the twentieth century. Writing in 1975, Nisbet offered this haunting description:

> Periodically in Western history twilight ages make their appearance. Processes of decline and erosion of institutions are more evident than those of genesis and development. Something like a vacuum obtains in the moral order for large numbers of people. Human loyalties, uprooted from accustomed soil, can be seen tumbling across the landscape with no scheme of larger purpose to fix them. Individualism reveals itself less as achievement and enterprise than as egoism and mere performance. Retreat from the major to the minor, from the noble to the trivial, the communal to the personal, and from the objective to the subjective is commonplace. There is a widely expressed sense of degradation of values and of corruption of culture. The sense of estrangement from community is strong.[1]

It is hard to read these words without taking them as a prescient sketch of our own time.

Some of this has been a matter of perception, to be sure, and part of what confounds us is that we know our sullen mood is not entirely justified. Generally speaking, this era has not been a time of cataclysm or disaster but of exhaustion and frustration. It has not been devoid of prosperity or opportunity, or of good news on many fronts; in fact, it feels peculiar in part because good news seems not to translate into confidence or hopefulness. What has really defined this twilight age has been a widespread failure to understand what is missing or what has gone wrong—a collapse of some of the preconditions for flourishing that we cannot quite explain to ourselves.

We are not only restless amid plenty, as Americans have always been. We are also awfully daunted by what on the surface seem like readily surmountable obstacles to our thriving together. This is in part because we underestimate our strengths. But it is also because we underestimate and misconstrue some of the problems we face. We lack the grammar and vocabulary to talk about what is breaking down, and so cannot even begin to do something about it. We look for diagnoses in the realms made visible to us by our assorted sciences of society, but the troubles we find there are not sufficient to justify our despondent mood. Something has gone wrong somewhere else, in some invisible realm, and we have been straining to perceive and describe what it might be.

This book is one such attempt to perceive and describe. It seeks some underlying causes of our unease and frustration—of the isolation that afflicts too many Americans, of the dysfunction that torments our politics, of the polarization that excessively sharpens both estrangement from some and affiliation with others, and of the resulting culture war that seems increasingly to be dividing us into two armed camps angrily confronting each other in every corner and crevice of American life. My goal is not to comprehensively explain all of these predicaments, needless to say. Nor is it even to outline the historical trajectory of our cultural evolution toward division and polarization—which others have done well in recent years, and which I have attempted in my own past writings too. Rather, the aim of this book is to highlight one particularly important cause that these distempers have in common—one that we tend to overlook.[2]

That cause is hiding in plain sight. Everybody knows that Americans have long been losing faith in institutions. That is a truism, if not a cliché. But what does it actually mean? Just what is an institution? What is involved in having faith in such a thing, and in losing that faith? And what is at stake? This book offers an inquiry into these questions, how they have played out in American life lately, and their implications for our future.

To describe this book as an inquiry is to say that it is moved by a set of questions more than by a set of answers. It is not a manifesto or a policy platform. It is more like a search for clues. And it is rooted in concern much more than in confidence.

That concern is a function of having witnessed the degradation of our common life in recent years from a peculiar vantage point. I am a scholar of politics and public policy at a think tank in Washington, DC, and the editor of a journal of political ideas. I have worked for a president of the United States, for a Speaker of the House of Representatives, and for various other politicians and policymakers. I labor these days among a group of analysts and activists who have been warning for most of this century that our politics has needed to turn its attention to the concerns of working families and insisting that there were constructive ways to do that. That perch has enabled me to witness close-up the deformations of our political life in this era: an extraordinary display of institutional failure and a kind of breakdown of social psychology that has spanned the ideological spectrum and transformed the political arena into a venue for a bitter and divisive culture war.

And that culture war has reached well beyond politics. In fact, it now pervades the arenas occupied by most of our core institutions, and it has been breaking down the barriers between them. It also utterly permeates the novel terrain of social media, which emerged in this century to great hopes that it might bring us together but has turned out to be an unparalleled setting for division and vitriol.

Looked at individually, each of these institutional breakdowns has the appearance of a failure of responsibility. Considered together, these failures must be seen as something more: a perverse distortion of what institutional responsibility means. As a practical matter, this has meant that the people atop one core institution after another—from our political and economic elites, to university administrators, to people with real power in the business and entertainment worlds, to too many religious leaders—have failed those who count on them and let our society down.

Our culture has responded to these disappointments with understandable anger and resentment. The populism of this moment in our politics is fundamentally antinomian, mistrustful of authority, and cynical about all claims to integrity. It looks to ease our disappointments by tearing down the institutions that embody them. And so our common life has come to be overrun with demolition crews of various sorts, promising to knock down oppressive establishments, to clear weeds and drain swamps and end infestations. They draw our attention to what we have too much of, and so distract us from what we have too little of. Today's populists have good reasons to be angry, but what they offer is insufficient.

Younger Americans have grown up bombarded with examples of institutional failure that tend to reinforce such attitudes. A country repeatedly disappointing itself is the only America they have known, and so they take it as a norm, not an exception. And now they see it culminating in a national politics that feels like a debauched rampage of alienation and dysfunction—depraved and degrading, corrupting everyone who goes near it, always finding surprising new ways to reach lower.

They are not happy about this, but their desire to overcome it expresses itself in various forms of rejection and dissent, rather than in a recommitment to the potential of our society and its institutions. Some are drawn to join the demolition crews, and those who are more naturally inclined to build are often left working without blueprints of what a more worthy alternative would look like. Their efforts are noble but unfocused and weak.

To do better, we will need to think about what we lack as well as what we want to rid ourselves of. And that means we will have to take up hard questions about the health and even the very purpose of the institutions of our society.

As we do that, we will repeatedly encounter a few threats to those institutions that are characteristic of our time, and that recur in one arena after another. We will find that the lure of cynical distance and of playing the outsider are deadly to the kind of renewal our society requires. We will notice that the culture of celebrity turns out again and again to be the enemy of a culture of integrity. We will see that our pervasive and polarized culture war is drowning our society in poisonous acrimony. And, perhaps above all, we will find that the people who occupy our institutions increasingly understand those institutions not as molds that ought to shape their behavior and character but as platforms that allow them greater individual exposure and enable them to hone their personal brands. A revitalization of a particular idea of what institutions are and do could be of help on all these fronts.

To warn of some dangers of our polarized age, however, is not to disclaim any party or point of view. I do not approach these questions as an outsider—and in truth no one does or could. I am a partisan myself. I'm a conservative, and I have spent my adult life articulating and advancing the ideals of the American Right. Like almost everybody on all sides, I am disappointed with my party these days, but I do not stand outside the fray. The inquiry I take up in this book is rooted in my conservative worldview, and while I try to love my party only a little more than it deserves (and am intensely critical of the leader it has chosen for itself these last few years), I have no doubt that what I offer here will be shaped, and at times also misshaped, by my deep-rooted views.[3]

The argument of this book is a conservative one of a particular sort. It begins from the premise that human beings are born as crooked creatures prone to waywardness and sin, that we therefore always require moral and social formation, and that such formation is what our institutions are for. This is, I think, a conservative premise without being a particularly partisan starting point. It is surely widely shared by readers elsewhere on the political spectrum, even if it is not what they emphasize. And because it is only the premise of an inquiry, it is a starting point for raising some questions and proposing some observations that might spark constructive responses, even from those who do not begin with my presuppositions and may not end up sharing my conclusions. My hope is that this book will leave you knowing not only more than you did when you started it but more than I did when I finished it—and that is likeliest to happen if we begin from different places.

Above all, though, I hope that what we learn together might move us to see that, while calling out the demolition crews may be an understandable response to the frustrations of our time, it is very far from enough. If we understand that a deformation of our expectations of institutions is at the core of our confusion and paralysis, we will grasp that we require a reformation of those institutions—and that this demands constructive work. Here, too, the words of Robert Nisbet in the mid-1970s can serve as something of a guide. "Just as twilight ages are a recurrent phenomenon of Western history," Nisbet wrote, "so are ages of social replenishment, of reinvigoration of social roots. Human beings cannot long stand a vacuum of allegiance."[4]

We are living in an era marked by a vacuum of allegiance. But the fact that we cannot long stand it does not tell us what to do. It is up to us to launch an age of social replenishment. That will require intellectual, cultural, political, spiritual, moral, and economic work. We each can have a part to play, if we want one. But, to begin, we have to see that such work is called for, and that it is not fundamentally a work of demolition.

For all our frustration and confusion, this is not a time for tearing down. It is a time to build.

PART I
A CRISIS OF DISSOLUTION

one

THE MISSING LINKS

W E AMERICANS ARE LIVING THROUGH A SOCIAL CRISIS. This is a straightforward fact, and easy to see. And yet part of this crisis, one of its symptoms, is that we can't seem to get a handle on just what it is that's wrong. It's sometimes even hard to tell whether the rage, foreboding, and despair that so often shape the national mood now are themselves the essence of the problem or are marks of a deeper dysfunction.

That mood is hard to miss. In our public life, it presents itself in bitter divisions, intractable frustrations, and an explosion of populist anger that crosses many demographic and partisan categories and seems to paralyze our system of government even as it energizes our politics. That anger has intensified with every recent national election, and it looks likely to transform our political priorities and expectations in some enduring ways.

In the realm of culture, too, frustration and hostility predominate, as various forms of identity politics, on both the Left and the Right, undermine the foundations of unity. Even our ability to carry on frank conversations has been degraded lately by a loss of trust and common ground. People often behave as though they cannot hold a set of facts and premises in common. In many cultural venues, professional settings, and academic environments, resentment and aggrievement seem to boil just under the surface, and some basic norms of open inquiry and mutual respect are under threat as a result.

But it's worse than that, because the problem is not just about how we talk to each other or take up public problems. The crisis is evident not only in our political and cultural interactions but in the personal lives of countless Americans, for whom hopelessness or alienation descends into outright despair. Although in some ways it is easier than ever to be in touch with others, ours is an era of unusual isolation and solitude. Generally speaking, American adults have fewer close friends, spend less time with others, and feel more disconnected today than they did a generation or two ago. And although it is easier than ever to be exposed to and informed by a wide range of views, Americans increasingly live in cultural and political bubbles, hearing only affirmations and elucidations of what they already believe.[1]

The effects of such isolation on our souls are hard to characterize, but they show up in a variety of distressing ways. Suicide rates have increased by almost 30 percent over the past two decades, according to the Centers for Disease Control and Prevention. The increase has been particularly steep in rural America and along the so-called Rust Belt, which runs from parts of Appalachia to the upper Midwest. In the very same regions, life expectancy has actually been going down. Economists Anne Case and Angus Deaton of Princeton University have attributed this decline to what they call "deaths of despair," linked to drug abuse, alcoholism, and suicide. This trend has been significant enough to drive the overall life expectancy of Americans down slightly in the past few years—the first sustained decline since the period from 1915 to 1918, when the First World War and a global flu pandemic killed untold millions.[2]

In many communities, these trends have been embodied in particular by an epidemic of opioid abuse that has laid bare an underlying scourge of isolation, desperation, and misery. About seventy thousand Americans died from overdoses of opioids in 2018. Many more live each day under the burden of addiction to these drugs. Opioids are used to dull pain, not to sharpen experience: they are sought as an escape from suffering.[3]

When you step back and listen, an awful lot of what's distinct about this moment in America seems like a reaction to a certain kind of suffering—a response to being left behind, disrespected, robbed of dignity and hope.

But why? None of us wants to look at suffering, breakdown, frustration, and anxiety and say we don't understand their origins. We often talk as though the reasons why our social fabric has grown so frayed are obvious. But what if they aren't?

Traditional economic concerns, a first resort for many social analysts, simply don't provide a sufficient explanation. Yes, we experienced a severe recession in 2007 and 2008, and the economy has been relatively sluggish for much of this century. In the immediate aftermath of the Great Recession, it would have been easy to say that the economic decline and the social breakdown were conjoined. But the trends then separated for an extended period, as the economy improved while isolation, drug use, political alienation, and other indicators of our broad social crisis did not. We have now actually been living through one of the longest economic expansions of the modern era. Even if that period of growth is now ending, the fact remains that it has persisted through this time of increasing political and cultural frustration. Unemployment has been very low, even in those regions where the social crisis seems to be most acute. Inflation is low too, as are interest rates, loan-default rates, and most other traditional economic warning signs.

The benefits of this period of modest growth have accrued unevenly across our society, but all parts of the income scale have seen improvements in this century. It's not that inequality and slow growth have not posed problems, only that they are nowhere near sufficient to explain the crisis that confronts us.[4]

Some other familiar measures of well-being, both absolute and relative, also fail to offer sufficient explanations. Crime is down, and we are safer than we have been in many decades. Some demographic groups have seen their health decline a little in this century, although in general Americans are healthier. But even those declines don't come close to explaining the source of people's anxiety (and as noted above, they actually seem to be symptoms as much as causes of a crisis of isolation and despair).[5]

In fact, some observers have argued that the frustration and anxiety that seem to overwhelm us are rooted in imaginary grievances and are themselves the problem. Harvard's Steven Pinker takes the complaints that roil our social life to be just irritable gestures of self-indulgent ingratitude. In a recent book, he reviews mountains of data on wealth, health, safety, and choice and concludes that populist outrage on all sides of our politics is detached from reality. And it is dangerous too, he says. "Indiscriminate pessimism can lead to fatalism: to wondering why we should throw time and money at a hopeless cause. And it can lead to radicalism: to calls to smash the machine, drain the swamp or empower a charismatic tyrant."[6]

But surely it is unreasonable to suggest that public frustration is just a kind of self-delusion—especially frustration that runs this deep and has revealed itself in such a broad range of symptoms. Pinker's happy data are not wrong, and neither are the economic statistics. But if these don't explain the reigning sentiments of our time, we should ask ourselves what such indicators might ignore, and what signs we might be missing.

In considering this question, we should be careful to distinguish causes from symptoms. When a patient presents at a doctor's office complaining of fatigue, the doctor doesn't just prescribe more sleep, though that might be part of the treatment. The doctor also considers, for instance, whether the patient might be lacking in iron. That kind of deficiency is not obvious directly from the symptom, but it can become apparent through a broader knowledge of the human organism.

We can say something similar here. The massive social crisis we confront—whether it's evident as populism or polarization or resentment or mistrust or a soul-crushing despair—clearly requires some direct responses. To treat it seriously, political leaders must listen to what people are asking for and help them get it. Our populist politics should not be ignored or wished away. And it is right that populism should reorder the nation's priorities some. But this explosion of frustration and resentment might also suggest that our society is in need of something it lacks but *isn't* asking for—and that the causes of our distemper run deeper than the symptoms. That is a challenge in a democracy. It is a challenge that requires us to consider what we know about the complex social organism that is a free society and not just what we hear each other saying in frustration.

So what do we lack but are not asking for? How would we even look for such an absence? We might begin by asking ourselves some questions: What does the missing thing look like? What is the nature of the deficiency we feel? What would it take to fill the gap? These kinds of questions begin to gesture toward a different sort of diagnosis. If the absence we are experiencing looks like isolation, mistrust, and alienation, then it is also a shortage of belonging, confidence, and legitimacy.

If that's the case, then it shouldn't surprise us that our traditional measures of wealth and health and personal freedom aren't raising alarms. These indicators, important as they are, assess our welfare individually. But we generally don't experience well-being alone. Flourishing happens in the joints of society—and this is also where the deepest sort of trouble shows itself.

In other words, many of our struggles seem rooted in relational problems. Loneliness and isolation, mistrust and suspicion, alienation and polarization—these are the characteristic maladies of this era. But because they are failures of sociality, they too often fall into the blind spots of our individualist culture.

This crisis of connectedness has been described in a variety of ways. A number of analysts across the political spectrum have argued that it must be ultimately philosophical or metaphysical—essentially that contemporary liberalism is so committed to the ideal of individual liberation that it lacks the conceptual framework to articulate ideals of solidarity or even of community. We depend on these deeper social foundations and yet we lack the tools to maintain or reconstruct them, and we have lost the words with which to speak about what we owe each other.[7]

Some, mostly on the Right, have suggested that at the core of the crisis is a collapse of family and religion—and that without these preconditions for individual flourishing we are uprooted and adrift. This would suggest our social crisis is a breakdown of tradition and moral order. Others, largely on the Left, have argued that, although simple economic measures of well-being cannot show us what is wrong, the trouble is still fundamentally material—that contemporary capitalism elevates the interests of the wealthiest above the rest, exacerbating inequality to the point that it becomes impossible for people to feel and function like equal parts of a greater whole.[8]

These sorts of diagnoses are all reasonably plausible, and they are also closer to each other than they sometimes seem. They treat the human person as embedded in a larger whole—be it metaphysical, moral, social, or economic—and they grasp that what is wrong has to do with the ways in which we now live out that embeddedness.

But although these ideas are helpful, they all share a definition of connectedness that still seems lacking. All essentially envision a kind of formless connection—people who are linked in principle or interacting one by one. They imagine American society as a vast open space filled with individuals—and so they call for ways of helping these people to link hands, be closer together, and share experiences and ideals.

This is the reigning, if generally implicit, metaphor of American social life. It accords with the individualism of our time even when it argues for community, and it feeds the sense that what we lack are connections and relationships. Thus we talk about breaking down walls or building bridges or casting a unifying vision to strengthen our society. We hope that social media might bind us together this way, or that the ideals of our politics will give us the conceptual framework for cohesion, or that our moral and religious traditions will reinvigorate our sense of solidarity, or that by narrowing the differences between rich and poor we will make our society more whole.

There is great appeal in this idea and in these different calls for solidarity. But something crucial is still lacking in this vision of connectedness. There is a missing step between joining together and recovering belonging, trust, and legitimacy. Formless connectivity does not get you there.

What we are missing, although we too rarely put it this way, is not simply connectedness but a structure of social life: a way to give shape, place, and purpose to the things we do together.

If American life is a big open space, it is not a space filled with individuals. It is a space filled with these structures of social life. It is a space filled with *institutions*. If we are too often failing to find belonging, legitimacy, and trust in our common life, then perhaps we are confronting not a failure of connection but a failure of institutions. Institutions do much more than connect us. Understanding our social crisis in terms of what they are and what they do could help us to see that crisis in a new light.

So just what is an institution? That question has actually been the focus of increasing attention in the social sciences of late. The last several decades have seen the emergence of a so-called new institutionalism in a number of fields, most notably sociology, economics, and political science. Taking distinct but related approaches, scholars in these fields have come to put the study of institutional behavior and decision-making at the center of their work. But they have not agreed on the precise meaning of the term.[9]

The breadth of the concept is evident in the range of definitions different scholars have offered. In his groundbreaking book *On Thinking Institutionally*, the political scientist Hugh Heclo reviewed various academic definitions of "institution" and stopped after cataloging well over a hundred. Some definitions describe institutions as collections of rules, norms, or even habits. Others incline to a more functional description that sees institutions as means of integrating people in the pursuit of social goals. Some see institutions as channels for power and ways of deploying authority. The various definitions are generally describing the same things, but the difference in emphasis matters. These distinctions result in part from the points of view of different academic disciplines and of schools within those disciplines. But they also get at the immense variety of roles that institutions play in any society. A concept so basic is inherently hard to define.[10]

Without dismissing those definitions, I will suggest a more straightforward one. Both because my own background is in political science and because our purpose here is especially to understand our social crisis in terms of institutions, I am drawn toward a definition that captures something of the breadth of purposes served by institutions. When I speak of institutions, then, I mean the durable forms of our common life. They are the frameworks and structures of what we do together.[11]

Some institutions are organizations and have something like a corporate form. A university, a hospital, a school, a legislature, a military, a company, and a civic association are all institutions. They are technically and legally formalized. But being an organization in this sense is not essential to being an institution.

Some institutions are durable forms of a different sort: they may be shaped by laws, norms, or rules but lack a corporate structure. The family is an institution; in fact, it is the first and foremost institution of every society. We can speak of the institution of marriage, or of a particular tradition or profession as an institution, or even of the rule of law. But that does not mean that rules are most fundamentally what institutions consist of either.[12]

While institutions come in a wide range of shapes and sizes, they share two distinct elements that, broadly speaking, may be said to unite them. That they are *durable* is essential. An institution keeps its shape over time, and so shapes the realm of life in which it operates. When it changes, it generally does so by incremental evolution of its shape and structure, not by sharp and disjunctive transformation, so that its form over time exhibits a certain continuity that is fundamental to what it is able to accomplish in the world.

Most important, each institution is a *form* of association. What's distinct about an institution is that it is a form in the deepest sense: a structure, a shape, a contour. But as Aristotle tells us, the form of a thing is at once distinguishable and inseparable from its materials or its substance. It is the shape of the whole, the arrangement that speaks of its purpose, its logic, its function, and its meaning. An institution, in this sense, is different from a group of people in the same way that a form is different from the matter of which it is composed—as, for instance, the shape of a candle is different from the raw wax of which it is made. The institution organizes its people into a particular form moved by a purpose, characterized by a structure, defined by an ideal, and capable of certain functions.[13]

The forms of the world around us impress themselves on our perception and imagination. They shape our understanding of the boundaries of our experience. And they give us an idea of what it means to form, to transform, to reform, to deform, to conform. This is how our institutions shape our social existence and our associational lives.

In other words, institutions are by their nature formative. They structure our perceptions and our interactions, and as a result they structure us. They form our habits, our expectations, and ultimately our character. By giving shape to our experience of life in society, institutions give shape to our place in the world and to our understanding of its contours. They are at once constraining and enabling. They are the means by which we are socialized, and so they are crucial intermediaries between our inner lives and our social lives. They are how the city and the soul come to shape each other, and in our free society they are essential to the formation of men and women fit to exercise that freedom responsibly.[14]

One of the most important ways that institutions accomplish this task of formation is by giving each of us a role and therefore a shape or form in the world. Healthy institutions often function as molds for the people inside them. We pour ourselves into our family, our community, our church, our work, or our school, and in so doing we begin to take the institution's shape. That shape then enables us to be more effective. It both protects us and empowers us to interact with others. We aren't just loose individuals bumping into each other. We fill roles, we occupy places, we play parts defined by larger wholes, and that helps us understand our obligations and responsibilities, our privileges and benefits, our purposes and connections. It moves us to ask how we ought to think and behave with reference to a world beyond ourselves: "Given my role here, how should I act?"

Such formation is not only how we raise children to understand their places in the world. It is something each of us needs all the time. It is how we gain and sustain the habits and assumptions, the networks and mental maps, that enable us to thrive and to be at once free and responsible. When it works well, it is how we can accumulate and replenish social capital, and how we gain an idea of virtue through habituation in the practice of virtue.

This term "social capital," which we will return to a few times, is metaphorical, of course. It describes the resources at our disposal to enable effective cooperation—the skills, habits, networks, and arrangements that make it possible for our society to hold together and for its members to benefit from it. It is a cold kind of metaphor and reeks of economics, but it has some value in describing the types of social problems we now frequently confront. A depletion of social capital and a failure to replenish it is one way to describe the challenges facing a lot of Americans today. As we'll see, these problems are the direct result of the wilting of our institutions. Social capital can be spent in a wide variety of ways—some more constructive than others. But it is most effectively built up and replenished through the formation that our institutions provide us.[15]

And yet, we rarely think of the necessity of institutions for such formation now. In fact, we rarely think of the necessity of such formation itself, even when we bemoan the social breakdown we confront. As a result, we often fail to grasp the ways in which institutional decay or deformation drive that crisis. We therefore also tend not to see how studying what our institutions are and what they do might help us better understand that crisis.

It could, for one thing, help us see why our troubles feel more dire than the familiar economic and social statistics would suggest. When we think about the challenges our society faces, we tend to think about the array of forces pressing on it—globalization or automation or polarization or populism or radical individualism or ethnic nationalism. Since we feel like our society is under great stress, we think the intensity of these external forces must be the reason. But in fact, what stands out about our time is not the strength of the pressures acting on our society. The history of our country has seen periods characterized by vastly more intense kinds of pressure. We now use "civil war" as a metaphor to illustrate rising cultural tensions, but it wasn't always just a metaphor. Even within living memory, our country has had to confront internal and external pressures that have objectively been far greater than those we face today.

We might worry about the fraying of liberal norms, but liberal democracy is not under the kind of stress today that it faced, say, in the 1930s or even the 1960s—eras of fascism and communism on the march abroad and intense political violence and cultural self-doubt at home. We rightly worry about racial tensions, but our cities are not burning. We complain about conflicts on university campuses, but no one is marching on administration buildings with automatic weapons. Look in on the America of the early 1970s, for example, and you'll find a society that seems to have had much bigger problems than we do. That's part of what leaves some people who are trying to diagnose our society so confused.

What does stand out about our time, though, is not the strength of the pressures we are under but the weakness of our institutions—from the family on up through the national government, with much in between. That weakness leaves us less able to hold together against the pressures we do face. It leaves all of us more uncertain about our places and less confident of the foundations of our common life. And it leaves us struggling with something like formless connectedness, a social life short on structural supports.

This barely describable formlessness can feel like freedom to people who have lots of social capital to spend, even as it feels like deprivation to those who don't. That difference, the sources of which are so often invisible to us, helps explain why nearly everything about the way we live now seems to exacerbate our inequalities, strengthening the strong while weakening the weak. And it has a lot to do with why a crisis of institutions would present itself perhaps most powerfully as a crisis of our inner lives—of despair and isolation, loneliness, and loss of purpose.[16]

Such social shapelessness is how we can be at once too confrontational and too lonely, in touch with everyone and yet untouched by anyone, alienated together. It is how everyone can claim the mantle of the outsider at the same time. It results from the lack of place, connection, and belonging that are functions not just of being alone but also of being adrift, denied roles that might help us fit as parts into a larger whole.

If what is distinct about our social crisis is the weakness of our institutions and the depletion of the interpersonal resources at our disposal, then the challenge we face is a challenge of institutional revival. And yet, at this moment, our politics and culture are horrifically ill-suited to such a renewal. Our age combines a populism that insists all of our institutions are rigged against the people with an identity politics that rejects institutional commitments and a celebrity culture that chafes against all structure and constraint.

This means the revival we want will require a real change of attitude and a new way of understanding the problems we face. Pursuing such a revival will require us to put some key questions about institutions front and center, which doesn't come naturally. The notion that we are formed by institutions runs against the grain of how we think about personal freedom, justice, choice, and many other things we care about. It amounts to a practical argument against a lot of liberal theories of man and society. Institutions play a role that we would rather believe is unnecessary. They form us by mediating between each of us and all of us, so our need for them suggests we need formation and mediation—and we would prefer to think we don't.

SUCH RESISTANCE IS NOTHING NEW, ESPECIALLY IN AMERICA. IT HELPS explain why we have always tended to be blind to institutions or to resist them. Our popular culture has its roots in a dissenting Protestantism that sought a direct connection to the divine and rejected as inauthentic or illegitimate most forms of institutional mediation. That culture has therefore always appealed to an implicitly individualistic conception of the human person as complete and whole, in need of liberation more than formation.

In the 1830s, Alexis de Tocqueville took account of this peculiar disposition, and observed that it extends well beyond specifically religious matters. Americans, he argued, hate to have anything stand between themselves and the subject of their thoughts or pursuits. "This disposition of their mind soon leads them to scorn forms, which they consider as useless and inconvenient veils placed between them and the truth."[17]

That desire for immediacy, informality, and authenticity is one of the most distinctly American facets of our national character. We pride ourselves on it. So even though Americans actually stand out as institution builders in practice—our Constitution is essentially an institutional outline, and we have a civil society teeming with institutions of all shapes and sizes—our national ethic is, in important respects, anti-institutional and always has been. The theory that shapes our self-understanding is at odds with our practice of social life, which leaves us struggling to explain and understand ourselves.[18]

We can see this in the ways in which we describe our own history. When progressives tell the American story, they often speak in terms of mass social movements crashing as waves upon our shores—notable particularly for their lack of institutional form. When conservatives tell the story, we tend to speak in terms of principles rather than institutions, and so we find in the American founding an intellectual achievement more than an institutional one. For all that we insist we love the Constitution, we tend to hate Congress and the presidency and the courts—and those *are* the Constitution.

Today, the Right tends to argue about the role of government in a fairly abstract manner—discussing its boundaries more than how its institutions should operate within those limits. Of course, in the age of Trump, the Right barely advances even that argument. Conservatives instead approach our institutions with extraordinary suspicion and hostility. The Left, meanwhile, is now increasingly drawn to identity politics, which is a politics both devoid of and hostile toward institutions. It attributes to people a place based on their biology or ethnicity, and so treats their unformed selves as nearly all there is to know.

Looking for ways to make a difference, younger Americans therefore tend to think in terms not of channeling their ambitions through institutions but rather of going around them. Because our politics has always rewarded those who can successfully claim the mantle of the outsider—now even more than usual—the temptation to approach our institutions antagonistically, or to avoid them altogether, has grown very strong. When we look for solutions, we tend to look not to institutions but to individuals, movements, ideals, or maverick outsiders.

Maybe what we resist most is the very idea that we would need to be formed by institutions at all. The liberal ideal of freedom, which has often been at the core of our political imagination, is rooted in the premise that the choosing individual is the foundation of our social order. Liberating that person—whether from oppression, necessity, coercion, or constraint—has frequently been understood to be the foremost purpose of our politics. Our parties have argued about how to do it and about what kind of liberation the individual most desires or requires. But they have agreed, at least implicitly, that once properly liberated, that person could be free.

There is of course a deeper, older idea of freedom that contends that, in order to be free, we need more than just to be liberated. We need to be formed for freedom—given the tools of judgment and character and habit to use our freedom responsibly and effectively. Such formation for freedom is a key part of what our institutions are for, starting with the family and spreading outward to the institutions through which we work, learn, worship, govern, and otherwise organize ourselves. But the idea that this should be required for freedom has never quite sat well with us, and so the idea that we need institutions never quite has either.

That our theories of ourselves downplay or resist institutions means there is an unusual and unhelpful distance between theory and practice in American life. It doesn't mean we do not rely on institutions; it means we don't have a language for describing them or our reliance on them. This can be fine when our institutions are strong, because it lets us benefit from them while believing we don't need them—and so allows us to feel even more free than we are. But when our institutions grow weak, our impoverished vocabulary means we lack the language for explaining to ourselves what has gone wrong and what to do about it. And our institutions have grown weak now.

Fortunately, our struggle for words to explain what has happened can itself provide some insight. When we do speak about our institutions, when we can't avoid the glaring problems that confront them, we speak about them in a particular way that we should be careful to notice. We speak in terms of a declining trust, respect, faith, or confidence in institutions.

It is worth our while to consider why we resort to these terms of fidelity and trust, which are actually quite a peculiar way to speak about institutions. In this telling choice of words may be a vital clue to how to better understand the crisis we face, and even to what we might do about it. What does it mean, then, that so many Americans say they have been losing confidence in our country's institutions?

two

FROM MOLDS TO PLATFORMS

THE PLUMMETING OF PUBLIC CONFIDENCE IN INSTITUTIONS over the past half century may be the most thoroughly corroborated finding in the study of American public opinion. There are just mountains of evidence for it. In fact, the sheer quantity of data and the breadth of the phenomenon the data demonstrate make it hard to attribute this collapse of trust to any simple set of causes.

Gallup, for instance, has kept track of Americans' confidence in various institutions for decades—in most cases from 1973 until today. The trend in its figures is unmistakable. From big business, banks, and the professions to the branches of the federal government, the news media, organized labor, the medical system, public schools, and the academy, confidence in our institutions has been falling and falling. In almost every case, the decline was gradual at first, through the 1970s and '80s, grew a little steeper in the 1990s, and then accelerated sharply in this century.

In the early 1970s, 80 percent of Americans told Gallup they had "a great deal" or "quite a lot" of confidence in doctors and hospitals, for instance. In 2018, the figure was 36 percent. Forty years ago, 65 percent of Americans said they had "a great deal" or "quite a lot" of confidence in organized religion, while in 2018 just 38 percent did. Sixty percent expressed confidence in the public schools back then, while just 29 percent did so in 2018. Even in 1975, a year after Richard Nixon's resignation in disgrace, 52 percent of Americans expressed confidence in the presidency, while in 2018 just a third of Americans did. Gallup found that 42 percent of the public had confidence in Congress in the 1970s. In 2018, that figure stood at a stunningly low 11 percent.

This pattern holds for nearly all the institutions Gallup asked about. A few, like the courts, have fallen less sharply in the public's estimation—and they have only really started falling in this century. And just one institution that Gallup has followed over that period—the military—is significantly more trusted today than in the 1970s (claiming the confidence of 74 percent of the public in 2018, compared to 58 percent in 1975). We will see what we can learn from that exception, but the overall trend is unmistakable, and not just in Gallup's data but in every available source of information on public views. The American people have gone from extraordinary levels of confidence in our major institutions to striking levels of mistrust.[1]

Part of the reason for this pattern is surely that Americans' faith in institutions was unusually high in the middle part of the twentieth century. Emerging from decades of social, cultural, and political consolidation and then the searing experiences of depression and war, Americans in the 1950s and early 1960s in particular had extraordinary confidence in the large institutions that dominated the life of the nation, and some of the subsequent decline in trust was a kind of normalization. But that doesn't explain the increasing intensity of that decline, or its acceleration in this century. Something more has been happening.

If we were to look at one institution or another on its own, it might be easy to come up with plausible explanations for this decline in trust. Some specific scandal, failure, or controversy could probably help explain each case. But to see that nearly all our institutions have been losing the public's trust at the same time is to recognize that deeper forces are at play, and that what has been happening might be best understood as a shift in how we think about institutions more generally.

This, in turn, should lead us to consider just what this idea of trust in institutions really is. What does it mean to have faith or confidence in an institution?

If, as I suggested earlier, institutions can be defined as the durable forms of our common life, then it follows that each institution works to accomplish some socially important task (say, educating the young, making laws, defending the country, serving God, helping the poor, producing some service or product, or meeting a need) by establishing a structure and process—a form—for combining people's efforts toward accomplishing that task. In effect, then, the institution also forms people so they can carry out that task successfully, responsibly, and reliably. It fosters an ethic that defines how they go about their common work, which in turn shapes their behavior and character. That ethic often involves a way of achieving the institution's core goal effectively while guarding against some of the dangers of social life—like individual selfishness, avarice, ambition, lust, or vice. This is part of what we value about our institutions: in addition to carrying out their intended work, they form people to do so appropriately, properly, and ethically.

We trust an institution, then, because it seems to have an ethic that makes the people within it more trustworthy. We trust political institutions when they take seriously their obligation to the public interest, and when they shape the people who work within them to do the same. We trust the military because it values courage, honor, and duty in carrying out the defense of the nation, and forms men and women who do too. We trust a business because it promises quality and integrity in meeting some need we have, and rewards its people when they deliver. We trust a university because it is devoted to the search for truth, and shapes those within its orbit to pursue that search through learning and teaching. We trust a journalistic institution when it holds itself to high standards of honesty and accuracy, and so renders the work of its people reliable.

We lose trust in an institution, therefore, when we no longer believe that it plays this ethical or formative role, serving as a forge of integrity for the people within it. One way this might happen is when an institution plainly fails to protect us, or even actively betrays our confidence, in the performance of its work—as when a bank cheats its customers or a member of the clergy abuses a child. In such situations, the institution is revealed to have been corrupted into serving those within it at the expense of its core purpose. Rather than shaping the people inside it, it comes to be deformed by them for their own ends. This is a betrayal by insiders—a mode of institutional corruption we might call "insiderism"—and it is perhaps the most obvious factor driving the loss of faith in institutions.

The gross abuses of power revealed over the past few years by the so-called #MeToo movement have shaken our confidence in some important institutions in just this way. Revelations of sexual abuse by Catholic priests and a subsequent cover-up by the institutions of the church have done the same. Political scandals that reveal financial corruption, abuses of power, or even just abject incompetence often work this way, and recent decades have unfortunately been full of them. In the business world, insiderism might happen when the pursuit of profits is plainly put above basic integrity or when institutions entrusted with enforcing the rules turn out to be breaking them (as when the accounting firm Arthur Andersen was found to have knowingly enabled gross corruption in the Enron scandal in the 1990s and early 2000s). In each case, insiders use their power over outsiders to gain advantage, and so violate professional codes, norms of integrity, or other institutional guardrails.[2]

It is obvious why corruption of this first sort should lead to a loss of trust. But it's also important to understand that this happens because institutions fail to meet the expectations we have of them: that they will perform crucial social functions with integrity and will shape people who do too. This kind of corruption is therefore also a form of hypocrisy, a failure to live up to commitments.

But this explanation for our loss of trust fails to account for the intensity of that loss in our time. Institutional corruption is not a new phenomenon and, needless to say, human moral frailty and sinfulness are not either. Ours is an age filled with examples of corruption, but so is pretty much every age. Institutions throughout our society have ways of addressing their own failures and perversions, and in some respects (especially in politics), we actually live in an era of less explicit corruption than we have seen in the past. Certainly, the insider corruption we do see is part of the problem. But something more is going on.

Alongside plenty of familiar insiderism, we have also seen in this century another less familiar form of institutional deformation. We might call it "outsiderism," and it involves institutions that fail to form men and women of integrity because they fail even to see such formation as their purpose. Rather than contain and shape individuals, these institutions seem to exist to display individuals—to give them prominence and gain them notice without stamping them with a particular character, a distinct set of obligations or responsibilities, or an ethic that comes with constraints. Such institutions prove unworthy of our trust not so much because they fail to earn it as because they appear not to seek or to desire it at all.

In fact, because this kind of institutional deformation is so prevalent, our very understanding of what institutions are for has been changing subtly but fundamentally. We have moved, roughly speaking, from thinking of institutions as molds that shape people's characters and habits toward seeing them as platforms that allow people to be themselves and to display themselves before a wider world. This subtle, gradual change in expectations has dramatically magnified our loss of trust in institutions.

When we don't think of our institutions as *formative* but as *performative*—when the presidency and Congress are just stages for political performance art, when a university becomes a venue for vain virtue signaling, when journalism is indistinguishable from activism—they become harder to trust. They aren't really asking for our confidence, just for our attention.

And in our time, many of our most significant social, political, cultural, and intellectual institutions are in the process of going through this transformation from mold to platform. The few exceptions prove the rule, because they tend to be the few institutions in which we aren't losing faith so quickly—again, the most notable of these is the military, which is also the most unabashedly formative of our national institutions. At the other end of the spectrum are many of the genuinely novel institutions of the twenty-first century: most notably the virtual institutions of social media, which are inherently intended as platforms and not molds. They are ways for us to shine and be seen, not ways for us to be transformed by an ethic shared with others. It would be strange to trust a platform, and we don't.

THERE IS, OF COURSE, A CERTAIN PERFORMATIVE ASPECT TO THE more traditional understanding of what institutions are for. We speak of them as giving us "roles" and "places" and "parts to play," and shaping us as a result. But those terms describe modes of modeling various kinds of integrity and of assuming obligations that ultimately structure our character. They describe roles within institutions, shaped by institutional standards that then shape the people playing those roles.

A person with a role defined by a position in a formative institution—an elementary school vice principal, a platoon commander, a Girl Scout—is playing that part, pouring himself or herself into it, and so taking on its shape. By contrast, the more performative approach to institutions we increasingly see involves people with an institutional position using it as means of being seen and heard in the larger society. Such people define their roles not against a standard intrinsic to the institution but as expressions of themselves, acting *on* institutions more than *in* or *through* them, and so in a sense remaining outsiders even while exercising institutional power.

Thus we find that many holders of elected office now spend much of their time participating in the cultural theater of our politics—often complaining dramatically about the corruption of the very institutions in which they hold positions—more than playing the role the system assigns them. We find many journalists leveraging the reputations of the institutions they work for to build their personal brands, outside of those institutions' structures of editing and verification, and to accumulate followers for themselves on social media. We find professors and scientists and ministers and CEOs and artists and athletes all using the legitimacy built up within professional institutions to raise their own profiles in a broader public arena, and often in ways intended to signal cultural-political affiliations more than institutional ones.

Sometimes people who engage in this kind of behavior are motivated simply by the desire to gain attention. But often they are also driven by a desire to participate in our increasingly all-consuming, wall-to-wall culture war. This conflict, which deforms our politics and increasingly pervades every facet of American life, is an inseparable element of the corrosion of institutional integrity by outsiderism. People frequently seek platforms in order to be seen taking the side of their tribe in these struggles. And as political and cultural polarization has intensified, the desire for such platforms has increasingly overtaken the desire to be formed and enabled, and therefore also constrained, by institutional responsibility. In some important institutions, this has led to the gradual replacement of a culture of integrity with something more like a culture of celebrity—in which achievement is measured by prominence and legitimacy by affirmation.[3]

There is a continuum between the mold and the platform, not a stark distinction. And the process by which people's perception of an institution changes from one to the other can be gradual and incremental. But as we increasingly come to assume that people working within institutions are using them to perform and to be seen, the underlying institutions become harder to trust. We are less ready to believe that these institutions are forming the people in them with integrity in mind, and so we don't think that the institutions are likely to advance a distinct and important social good while preserving against harm.

In fact, as different institutions come to be seen (by both the people in them and the larger public) as platforms for displaying individuals, they also come to lose their distinctions from one another and so tend to become homogenized into increasingly interchangeable stages for the same sorts of cultural-political performances. Their distinctive integrities, each shaped by a unique professional code, organizational history, or communal ethos, meld together and leave the complex institutional topography of our society more flat and barren. In this way, a culture at war with itself comes to be at war everywhere, so that, for instance, the worst facets of college-campus culture (where performative outrage sometimes overtakes academic investigation) are now apparent throughout our political, media, and business cultures too. It isn't quite that the culture of one institution has invaded others as that the boundaries and distinctions have broken down and everyone, inside and outside, is participating in the same obnoxious quarrel.

In the process, the boundaries between the internal lives of institutions and the public life of our society are also blurred, again encouraging insiders to act like outsiders and renege on their responsibilities—to seek the benefits of institutional positions while shirking the obligations they impose. Institutions understood as platforms cannot easily hold people accountable to one another, or to a larger common cause or ideal. We can't just trust a person on a platform with great power: without institutional structures to shape and constrain that person's behavior, corruption becomes hard to avoid.

This process undermines our confidence in institutions from two directions. On the one hand, people outside the institution—people who need it, or interact with it, or observe it—lose respect for the institution as they come to think of it mostly as a means for the personal promotion of those within. On the other hand, people within the institution forget the value of whatever constraints it might impose on them and come to understand it as a platform for themselves. From one direction we find a loss of respect for authority, process, integrity, and expertise, and from the other a loss of responsibility, restraint, and regard for a code of conduct. Each magnifies the other.

This change of attitude, this decline in the expectation that our institutions should be formative, is at the heart of our loss of faith in them. It is therefore also at the heart of our broader social crisis— because institutions understood as platforms rather than molds are less able to offer us objects of loyalty, sources of legitimacy, and the means of building mutual trust and connection. They can become venues for acting alone, more than together, and they therefore contribute to the sense of alienation and detachment that pervades our social life, rather than helping us address and overcome it.

THIS TRANSFORMATION OF EXPECTATIONS AND OF THE CHARACTER OF our institutions has not come out of nowhere. It has been driven by the same forces that have underlain the broader evolution of our society over the past half century and more and that have been seen in different forms throughout the West in that time. As we have come to put less value on unity, to say nothing of conformity, and to put more value on individual self-realization, we have become ever more resistant to the ideal of the formative institution. As we have called upon each American to become more fully himself or herself, we have implicitly put aside the notion that our social institutions exist to shape us.[4]

Meanwhile, over the decades, our popular culture has increasingly become a celebrity culture, in which exposure, prominence, audience, and the appearance of authenticity are paramount. In many domains of American life, this has tended to blur the distinction between reality and image, and this logic could hardly have avoided penetrating our core institutions.[5]

In our public life, at the same time, democratization and transparency have been wielded as tools of purification. And while their benefits have been widely touted, their countervailing costs have been almost entirely ignored. As we will find in the coming chapters, those benefits are real and vital, but the costs can be enormous—especially if they are ignored. Transparency is a necessary guard against insiderism, but in excess it can easily rob an institution of any inner life, and so can naturally leave people holding institutional roles with the impression that performing for an outside audience is all they're doing.

As this has happened, a kind of intellectual democratization, making specialized knowledge more easily available to all (especially on the internet), has sown widespread doubt of many forms of professional authority—of the physician, the scholar, the scientist, the journalist, the expert of any kind. Such skepticism is sometimes justified, of course, but sometimes it is not, and it is precisely the forms of institutional integrity that are supposed to help us tell the difference. They are what might separate the expert from the charlatan in many fields. Much of what we have understood in recent years as a growing inability to agree on what is true, or to distinguish fact from fiction, is rooted in this revolt against expertise.

The polarization of our society—which is not only political but also cultural, economic, educational, and spiritual—has played a central role in driving these trends too. By simultaneously fragmenting our institutions and driving Americans to cohere into more or less two large masses, it has created the circumstances for the culture war that so many of us find impossible to avoid. Both economic inequality and cultural bifurcation have pushed this polarization along, and the two have been much related.

These causes are of course thoroughly intertwined. They are just a few facets of the story of our society's evolution over the past half century or so—an evolution that in many important respects has been for the good, but that has come with downsides that our politics is now forced to reckon with. And while it has been driven by these factors, the growing deformation of key institutions has itself also been a facet of this evolution and so has further accelerated its other elements.

To chart these causes is not to say that before they were set in motion there was some golden age in which American institutions were simply strong and constructive. Institutional deformities reflect broader societal deformities. So in eras shaped by chaotic social change, our institutions were often unstable. In eras of intense stratification or injustice, key institutions were frequently part of the problem. In eras of overbearing cohesion and consolidation, our institutions tended to exhibit a certain gigantism. Addressing these problems, to the extent they were addressed, meant institutional reform, as we have seen in every age of social change in our history. The problems now evident in our core institutions are similarly facets of broader social realities, and they may be addressed not by a return to some past era of supposed tranquility or vigor but by responding to the challenges embodied in institutional deformations. That means we must first come to terms with these challenges and consider how we each might help address them.

This transformation of our understanding of the role of institutions is therefore obviously not the one and only cause of our broad social crisis. But it is the cause to which we tend to be most blind, so it is worth the effort to more fully understand it. It also points toward an answer to one of the deepest quandaries that confronts us now.

When we look at our challenges today, we often notice that addressing them seems like it would require a return or a reversal—a recapturing of something lost that seems as impractical as unscrambling eggs. This leaves us thinking that recovery may be impossible. It contributes to the despair that now so often prevails in our social commentary and to the blinding nostalgia that afflicts our politics. But the idea that what we require is reversal is itself, in part, a function of failing to think institutionally—of failing to grasp the real structure and character of human society.

The fact is that what we need is not reversal but renewal. Renewal is always a possibility, because our social life is generational. The rising generation is only starting out, and young people can receive their inheritance as either a burden or a resource. It can be a resource if it gives them the means to thrive, rather than just debts to pay. These means can be material, like wealth and infrastructure. But they are above all moral and spiritual. The young have the energy that the old too often lack; they have the ambition that the old have spent, the hope the old have either realized or depleted. What they lack is formation—and that is what renewal requires too.

But although renewal is always possible, it does not happen by itself. It depends on some essential preconditions. Some of these are structural or supportive. Renewal requires safety, order, law, justice, and freedom. It requires avenues to dignity and legitimacy, intimacy, friendship, honor, pride, truth, and love. But some of these preconditions are moral or formative. Renewal requires that the rising generation, and that every generation in society, be socialized and moralized and formed to thrive—that we all be made better and more capable of reaching our potential.

We often speak of renewal as though it were a matter of social transformation. And it is in part. But at its core it is a matter of personal transformation. Enduring progress happens soul by soul, but that is actually why it can only happen through the institutions of society, which touch and form each of us. We are always in need of personal formation, which we ironically cannot hope to get on our own. Or, to put this in the colder, more generic terms of contemporary social science, the secret to renewal is the generation and replenishment of social capital by the right kinds of socialization. This is the great difficulty that confronts us now: How can we make people better able to benefit from the advantages this kind of society offers them and better able to overcome the disadvantages this kind of society imposes on them? The answer is a matter of personal formation much more than social reform—or rather, it is a matter of understanding social reform as geared to personal formation.

Crucial to such understanding is the idea that institutions should be formative—and that they should act as links between the personal and the social. What we need, then, is a recommitment to such an understanding of institutions. Our challenge is less to calm the forces that are pelting our society than to reinforce the structures that hold it together. That calls for a spirit of building and rebuilding, more than of tearing down. It calls for approaching broken institutions with a disposition to repair so as to make them better versions of themselves. And it calls for a willingness to adopt a new attitude toward the various social forms in which we are each embedded.

Seeing that could help us better understand our social crisis, and it can also give us some things to do about our social crisis—some steps that just about any of us can take to make things better. We can each contribute something by approaching key institutions differently, in ways small and large, day in and day out. That's not a matter of changing public policy or demanding grand reforms or protesting against corruption and abuses of power. There's an important role for each of those things. But there is also an important role for understanding ourselves as formed by institutions and acting accordingly—for asking ourselves, in little moments of decision, "What should I do here, given my role or my position?" As a parent, a teacher, a police officer, a scientist, a senator, or a pastor, what is my responsibility in this particular situation?[6]

And there is a dire need, as well, for men and women at every level in each of our society's institutions to channel their energies into that institution's objectives and purposes—defining their ambitions by its distinct modes of integrity, seeing its aspirations as theirs, adopting its ethos for their own, and understanding its boundaries and not just its powers as formative. In other words, we should want to see and strengthen internal parties of the institutions—a party of the university, of the legal profession, of the Congress, of the league, of the church or congregation—which are distinct from the parties to our politics, and which cut across them. Such parties could help some of our institutions function more like diverse sanctuaries from the culture war than interchangeable battlefields in it. Each of these parties can be defined by its distinct purpose and character and seek to improve its institution in its own terms, rather than in broader political or cultural terms. Our society does not have to be one big "yes" or "no" question over which we are constantly at each other's throats. It can consist of a diversity of ends pursued by a diversity of means, united by some crucial common ideals.

None of this can hope to be fully apparent in the abstract, of course. Having sketched the challenge's conceptual contours, we need to see it embodied in practice, in examples drawn from some of the most important institutions of our society, and then to consider its meaning.

PART II
INSTITUTIONS IN TRANSITION

three

WE THE PEOPLE

THE DEFORMATION OF OUR EXPECTATIONS OF AMERICAN institutions is evident from top to bottom in our society. Our tour of examples could begin anywhere from the interpersonal to the international. But it may be most reasonable to start with a particularly prominent form of the problem, and in an arena where no one could deny that serious dysfunction exists: the institutions of our national government and politics.

Despite our long tradition of demeaning the political, we Americans probably identify ourselves with our particular political institutions to a greater degree than do citizens of any other nation of the world. Our country was founded in an act of political separation that was rooted in institutional as well as philosophical arguments, and by 1788 we had adopted a Constitution that established the basic institutional framework by which we still govern ourselves. We can hardly understand ourselves apart from it. As the historian Hans Kohn put it, "The American Constitution is unlike any other: it represents the lifeblood of the American nation, its supreme symbol and manifestation. It is so intimately welded with the national existence itself that the two have become inseparable."[1]

One of the implications of this deep identification with the structure of our regime is that patterns of cultural change have often found themselves reflected in the functioning of our political institutions. Unity and conflict, chaos and order, cohesion and fragmentation in American life have always imprinted their likenesses upon the workings of our government. We can discern our condition in theirs. And this time is no different.

IN TRACING THAT PATTERN, WE SHOULD BEGIN WITH CONGRESS—because the Constitution begins there and because in a lot of ways the strange decay of our political institutions has been evident first and foremost in Congress.

It is perfectly obvious that something has gone wrong with Congress in our time. In one respect, the intensity and energy of the institution are very high at present: Congress is the scene of constant dramatic confrontations and what seem like epic battles—fights over confirmations of judges and other officials, budget showdowns, heated oversight hearings, and more. But in other respects, Congress is doing next to nothing. There hasn't been a proper budget process in over a decade, very little significant legislation gets passed, and most members serving today have never really been part of a traditional legislative process. This juxtaposition of intensity and incapacity amounts to a profound dysfunction. Whether you measure it by legislation, public approval, member satisfaction, or even just the volume of committee work or each house's ability to live by its own procedures, the Congress now looks to be in disarray.

And the primary reason for that dysfunction may be the worst news of all: Congress is weak because its members want it to be weak. Their behavior and priorities reflect a peculiar lack of institutional ambition.

Institutional ambition among legislators is essential to the functioning of the American system of government. The Constitution gives Congress powers but not responsibilities. The president is required to execute the laws. The courts are required to interpret them. But while the general scope and reach of Congress's powers are laid out in Article I, the institution is not really told what it has to do within that scope. The assumption was that Congress would run as far and as hard as the Constitution allowed, so only boundaries were required.

That assumption is made plain in the writings of the framers. James Madison, in particular, thought it a basic premise of politics that "in republican government, the legislative authority necessarily predominates." He expected that Congress would exhibit an unquenchable ambition and would always be, in his words, "extending the sphere of its activity, and drawing all power into its impetuous vortex." The legislative branch would be so dominant because its members would speak most directly for the public, and their roles could not be restricted by laws as the job of a judge or a president could be. They would have the power to make those laws, after all, and so to direct the immense power of government. Congress's power had to be divided between two houses and shared at the margins with the other branches to keep this overbearing legislature from taking advantage of the weakness of those other branches.[2]

This strikes our modern ears as a little bizarre. It seems to get things backward. The legal academy and American political science have for many decades been occupied with debates about the rise of the imperial executive, the activist judiciary, and the administrative state, all of which have amassed their power at Congress's expense. Presidential power has ballooned, as has the reach of the courts. But we tend to underplay the degree to which this has happened as the result of willful congressional dereliction, and to overlook some of the ways that this dereliction has transformed the character of Congress as an institution.

Sometimes such dereliction is a simple matter. Members of Congress don't want to make hard choices or bear the responsibility for trade-offs, and so they keep the easy calls for themselves and let the president, or at times judges, make the tough ones. This means Congress passes vague legislation that sets out popular general goals but then expects the executive branch to figure out the details of achieving them and lets judges sort out the complicated problems that result. We can see this pattern in recent years in health care, education policy, environmental policy, immigration, and across a wide range of other issues. It is a decidedly bipartisan vice.

This kind of delegation of responsibility is not a new phenomenon. It has been building since at least the middle of the twentieth century, and in some respects well before that too. There now exists a well-developed framework of procedures and agencies for enabling it. There has also been some backlash against it, especially on the Right, though for the most part not in Congress. In the conservative legal culture, and among some judges, momentum is building for pushback against the delegation of legislative authority.

In this century, however, we have seen a powerful additional source of dereliction and dysfunction, which takes us deeper toward the core of Congress's institutional confusion. Simply put, many members of Congress have come to understand themselves most fundamentally as players in a larger cultural ecosystem, the point of which is not legislating or governing but rather a kind of performative outrage for a partisan audience. Their incentives are rooted in that understanding of our politics and not really in legislating. They remain intensely ambitious, as politicians always are, but their ambition is for a prominent role in the cultural theater of our national politics, and they view the institution of Congress as a particularly prominent stage in that theater—a way to raise their profiles, to become stars in the world of cable news or talk radio, to build bigger social media followings, and to establish themselves as celebrities.

Alexandria Ocasio-Cortez, a young Democratic congresswoman from New York, has offered one instance of this pattern since her election in 2018. She has proven exceptionally adept at getting attention, not only by outraging Republicans through expert trolling and a keen sense of how to rev up social media energy, but also by using fellow Democratic politicians as props in morality tales about corruption and incumbency intended for her party's most energetic activists. As *National Journal*'s Josh Kraushaar noted in 2019, such behavior involved "garnering her limitless national attention at the expense of more mundane congressional work." Angering her own party's leaders might not normally be wise, Kraushaar continued, but "in a world where virality is more valuable than legislative productivity, it's unlikely her decisions will cause immediate political backlash. She's become an instant celebrity, an asset that often is short-lived though it pays huge political dividends while it lasts."[3]

Matt Gaetz, a young Republican congressman from Florida, offers another example. He has made a name for himself as a sharp and quotable combatant on cable television, always ready to chime in on any outrage of the moment. When a reporter from *Buzzfeed* asked him in 2018 whether he was concerned that he was gaining notoriety rather than prominence by doing this, his answer was, "What's the difference? People have to know who you are and what you're doing if your opinions are going to matter." It's hard to imagine a clearer illustration of the institutional transformation we are tracing here, and many other examples can be found now in the ranks of both parties in Congress.[4]

That transformation is precisely a change from mold to platform. Congress, like any serious institution, functions by socializing its members to work together. By establishing rules and norms, avenues to recognition and status, and a commitment to the strength and purpose of the institution itself, it gives shape to a type of human be-ing and citizen who can be called a member of Congress. For much of our history, newly elected members would be gradually formed into this distinct type over the course of their time in the institu-tion—bringing their individual points of view, priorities, strengths, and weaknesses to the table but using them to fill out the role of the legislator, to pour themselves into it and take its shape. This had its downsides. It frustrated efforts to reform Congress, and it created some distance between members and the public they represented. But it also yielded great benefits—forming legislators who would play their assigned role in our system.

This kind of socialization is essential not only to enable legislation and accommodation but also to keep the enormous power of the national government in check. By shaping and channeling the ambi-tions of its members, Congress sets them up to counteract ambitious presidents and judges. As Madison put it, "The interest of the man must be connected with the constitutional rights of the place." Mem-bers who allow themselves to be molded by Congress take the shape required by the place that the legislature is assigned in our system, and they make its interests their own.[5]

But when those members look to the institution as a means of displaying themselves rather than letting it form their character and ambitions, they do not become socialized to work together. They act like outsiders commenting on Congress, rather than like insiders participating in it. Much of what they say and do, even in private dis-cussions with colleagues, is intended not for their peers but for an out-side audience that wants to see a dramatic enactment of culture-war animosity. They often don't much care what other legislators think of them, because their standing and prospects don't depend on their colleagues and because they are not engaged in common work but in a spectacle put on for others. This engenders a distorted set of virtues and abilities: a form of courage that involves being willing to anger other politicians in order to cater to a small group of devoted outside followers and a form of professionalism that is about sticking to the livid cultural script rather than playing an accommodating constitutional role. Such members try to gain status and prominence by endlessly scorning the institution they worked so hard to enter.

This sort of attitude was particularly prominent among Republicans in the Obama years but has thoroughly spread to the Democrats in the Trump years, so that both parties now evince it. It has been driven in part by a centralizing tendency in Congress that has put nearly all of the power to set the agenda and move legislation in the hands of a small group of leaders in each house, leaving most other members with little real legislative work to do much of the time. Meanwhile, changes in the cultural and media environments surrounding the political system have made melodramatic outrage the coin of the realm. Members consequently use more and more of their time and energy to build a personal brand and excite fans and followers.

This is exacerbated further by the loss of protected spaces for deliberation in Congress, the importance of which cannot be overstated. Every institution needs an inner life—a sanctum where its work is really done. This is especially true in a legislature, where members must deliberate and bargain to reach practical compromises. But Congress has progressively lost that inner life, as all of its deliberative spaces have become performative spaces, everything has become televised, and there is less and less room and time for talking in private. By now, the leadership offices around midnight as a government shutdown approaches are the only protected spaces left, so it is hardly surprising that this is where a great deal of important legislation gets made.

All of this has happened in the name of transparency. And transparency is a good thing. Without it, institutions that serve a public purpose can easily become debased and unaccountable. There is no shortage of evidence for that. But every good thing is a matter of degree, and we have treated transparency as a good thing with no costs, when in fact it can have enormous costs that have to be accounted for. In this case, the price can be measured in institutional incoherence, and the result of ignoring it is a Congress that increasingly has the appearance of a show.

The push for transparency in Congress, which gained steam especially in the 1970s, was a response to congressional intransigence in the face of social change, and to undeniable insiderism and corruption in the institution. Beginning with the large post-Watergate class of freshman Democratic members in 1975, rules and norms governing seniority were overturned, and the inner workings of the institution were exposed to the sun for the first time. In 1979, a new cable network called C-SPAN began televising live all floor activity in the House of Representatives. By the mid-1980s, Senate floor action was also televised, as were many committee hearings in both houses.

The case for transparency was broadly persuasive, and it would be hard to deny that it has done great good. But some far-seeing observers on all sides of the political spectrum warned early on of the potential side effects of pushing too far in this direction. Legislative work would be impossible without some privacy to negotiate, they cautioned, and forcing everything Congress does into the open would be an irresistible invitation to grandstanding.[6]

Four decades later, these concerns seem awfully prescient. The argument for transparency still strikes with great force, and there is no question that the dangers of the (now mostly metaphorical) smoke-filled room—where power is exercised out of sight and without accountability—are real and serious. But so is the need for some private spaces for deliberation, bargaining, and dealmaking. When an institution becomes too thoroughly transparent, it becomes indistinguishable from the open public space around it, and so it is simply another platform for public speech rather than a structure for meaningful action. Of course this is exactly what has happened in Congress—as a penchant for transparency unbalanced by a sense of its costs, combined with the fragmentation of the media and the polarization of our politics, has undermined its capacity to fulfill its crucial role.

In fact, this transformation now often obscures from us the very nature of that role, so that even proposals for reforming Congress frequently miss the mark. Many reformers are moved by frustration with the slow pace of legislation or with the multitude of choke points that prevent decisive action. So they argue for reforms that would move Congress in the direction of a parliamentary model, where the majority party is more fully empowered to enact its will. A legislature guided by this purpose (particularly in a two-party system, where majorities are not the products of coalition bargaining) can accommodate quite a lot of grandstanding, since it is not fundamentally a dealmaking arena. It is where a majority party does what it promised its voters it would do while the minority huffs until the next election.

The purpose of Congress in our system, however, is not to empower the majority but to compel accommodation in an often fractured society. Ours is decidedly not a parliamentary system, not only in a basic structural sense but also in terms of its core purpose. Our Constitution restrains the exercise of political power to help ensure that only the will of broad, durable majorities can be acted upon. Narrow and ephemeral majorities (which are the only kind that our elections have produced for a generation) are not enough. Reforms intended to move Congress toward a parliamentary approach—like the elimination of supermajority requirements and the stricter enforcement of party discipline—would not help the Congress envisioned by the framers of our Constitution work better but would alter its essential character, and in ways that would trample minorities and make durable accommodations less likely. They are not the answers to the troubles that bedevil today's legislature.

Rather, reformers should see their goal as a Congress that enables, and indeed compels, accommodations. We need that in our time perhaps even more than usual. Our political culture is particularly bad at finding durable compromises now. It is even bad at pursuing them—at forcing political actors to face the reality that people with whom they disagree aren't going away, to confront the unavoidable need for trade-offs, and to recognize that politics in our democracy is more of a tug of war than a fight to the death.[7]

A functional Congress could be of great help on that front. But an institution geared toward enabling accommodation and compromise would have to allow for more private deliberation, create more rather than fewer power centers, treat conflict and debate as signs of health rather than failure, and give legislators much more to do so that their pride and ambition become intertwined with the institution—moving them to insist on its prerogatives within our larger system of government and shaping them to suit Congress's contours and aims. We badly need a party of the Congress within each legislative chamber, a cohesive group of members of both political parties who prioritize the institution's pride of place, insist on reinforcing its norms and defending its centrality, and see themselves as operating within the legislature rather than acting on top of it.

In the absence of such institutionalism, members increasingly behave like outsiders and the institution lacks defenders and practitioners. Everyone can see this is a problem. Members of Congress are dissatisfied. They're unhappy with how the institution works, and their voters are too. So the opening for institutional reform may well exist. But a framework for effective changes would have to begin with a sense of what has gone wrong and what is missing. It would need to be rooted in a sense of Congress as a formative institution—

formative, that is, of its members. The resulting institutional identity and ambition could help members see that a stronger Congress is in their interest.

The shortage in Congress of institutional ambition—and of members willing to be unabashed insiders—is an enormous problem for the constitutional system and has to be the focus of efforts to improve and strengthen that system.

THE SAME IS TRUE NOW OF THE PRESIDENCY. IT MIGHT SEEM STRANGE to say so, since we are certainly not used to thinking of the executive branch as lacking ambition. But it has come to lack a properly constitutional ambition in a way that is highly relevant to the broader problem we are tracing here. Our presidents, like many members of Congress, now too often see themselves as outsiders yelling about the government more than insiders wielding its power. This has become especially clear under President Donald Trump, though it began well before him.

The Trump presidency has made the problem clearer because Trump, in an unusually explicit way, approaches politics in performative, theatrical terms. He exhibits an ambition to put himself at the center of our national consciousness and attention even more than to use the institutional power of the presidency to pursue policy goals. He expresses himself almost always as an outside voice speaking at, not for, the institutions of the government.

To say President Trump has sought to dominate our attention is not just to say that he has a big ego. He does, of course, but so do most politicians, especially at the highest levels. Surely everyone who runs for president runs at least in part to *be* something—even to be the most famous man or woman in the world. But they also run to *do* something. Trump wanted to do something too, but how he has understood and pursued that desire might be what makes his particular ambition most distinctive.

A politician seeking high office naturally thinks about how to be something by doing something—how to use his office to advance his aims and therefore also to win recognition and admiration. The framers of our Constitution understood that ambition would work this way and were acutely aware that the desire for fame and renown would speak powerfully to would-be leaders. They designed the institutions of our government to channel this desire in various ways. The ambitions of our presidents have generally been routed accordingly—driving them to work either through the system as it was conceived or against it in ways that are highly aware of (if also frustrated by) its structure.[8]

President Barack Obama, for instance, routinely attempted to exceed the bounds of presidential power, but he did it by seizing the powers of the legislative branch (in immigration policy, for instance) or by pushing the limits of more ordinary presidential powers (as in his uses of regulatory power). Trump's exertions in office have, for the most part, been of a different sort altogether. They have generally been neither channeled through the constitutional framework nor exactly directed against it, so that his ambition has barely been shaped at all by the imperatives of constitutionalism. His efforts have instead been conceived more as turns in the plot of the drama of our politics, aimed at driving the story, particularly the cable-news story.

This is in part because Trump has not been subject, as his predecessors were, to the formative power of our political institutions. Every one of our past presidents was formed by a set of institutions—as either a senior military officer or (much more frequently) a government official serving in other offices—that shaped his understanding of how to act effectively as the head of the executive branch. Donald Trump is the first American president who has not been shaped by any experience in such institutions. His life experience involved running a family business in real estate and then becoming a professional celebrity, essentially playing the part of a successful real-estate developer in American popular culture. He entered politics as another performance in that role and was elevated to the presidency thanks to his great success in playing it.

Trump's formative institutional experiences therefore shaped him to thrive in an era of politics as entertainment. In just about every setting, he has been acting for an audience, in the presidency no less than before his election. That helps explain his obsession with ratings and audience size, his running commentary on Twitter, and his peculiar tendency to comment on his own speeches as he delivers them. He, too, behaves like an outsider and so neglects the responsibilities of the insider. He can frequently be found complaining on social media about some action taken by the Justice Department—in other words, by his own administration—and echoing the terms and sentiments of media analysts as though he were simply observing our system of government.

The trouble, then, is not that the president has a grand sense of himself and his office. That has always been with us. The president is our head of state, as well as our head of government, so some degree of pomp has always accompanied the role, and its occupants have never lacked for self-regard. But a perception of the presidency as a stage occupied by an outsider speaking at and about our system of government rather than for it, a kind of commentator in chief rather than a political actor, is a newer and more ominous phenomenon.

Trump's immediate predecessor, Barack Obama, paved the path toward a celebrity presidency and was at times even more impatient with the contours and constraints of the office (though, as noted, he was also more aware of them). We have also seen this pattern of behavior in campaigns for some time—including in presidential campaigns. It would not be hard to show that a significant number of the people who ran for president in this century entered their party's primaries to raise their media profiles, without any real expectations of winning or serving. Like many members of Congress, they approached politics as a path to prominence and visibility. But the trouble has mounted with time, and it has contributed to a transformation of the character of our national politics. The barriers between politics and entertainment have become blurred in some disorienting ways as a result.

A telling instance of this pattern took place at a Trump rally in Florida in the summer of 2018. As the president delivered a characteristically bombastic address, CNN reporter Jim Acosta—a frequent and hostile critic of Trump's and also a regular target of the president's ire on Twitter and elsewhere—was speaking live on the air when a group of rally attendees began screaming epithets at him and making wild (perhaps threatening) gestures behind him on camera. Acosta seemed taken aback, later telling a CNN colleague that President Trump was "whipping these crowds into a frenzy to the point where they want to come after us."

But as several other journalists present at the rally later noted, after Acosta's on-air appearance concluded and he walked off of the CNN camera stand, some of the same rally attendees approached him to shake his hand, get his autograph, and take selfies with him, and he gladly obliged. As another reporter described the scene,

> Acosta began signing autographs. A slip of paper here, a campaign sign there. Even the bill of one "Make America Great Again" hat. Eventually one of his most persistent hecklers—a young man with a long, scruffy beard, wearing a MAGA cap backwards and a MAGA flag as a cape—engaged Acosta in a friendly conversation. By the end of the exchange, the Trump fan was begging Acosta for an on-air shoutout.[9]

Acosta and the protestors (and the president too) had been act-ing their parts in the dramatic scene, and at some level they all grasped that and could implicitly acknowledge it after the fact. This dynamic is perhaps most analogous to a WWE wrestling match: an event made to look like an athletic competition but that is in fact partially scripted and entirely performative. Our national politics in this century has increasingly fallen into this pattern, and it has proven more and more difficult to distinguish between fact and fic-tion, between reality and scripted drama.

Partisan observers—voters and citizens—have been willing to play their frantic, angry parts alongside the entertainer-politicians. They're not simply pretending. They really are angry, and they are eager to see how the people onstage do. But they are partially pre-tending—or at least most of them are. Now and then, someone will turn out not to have been in on the joke and so will be moved by what he sees on cable news to fire a handgun at members of Con-gress playing baseball or to turn up at a Washington pizzeria with a rifle. The rest of us might do a little better at distinguishing the most outlandish conspiracies and provocations from real outrages. But it does get harder all the time, and we live with a vague sense of unease about drawing distinctions between what people say and do and what they mean and intend. The moral logic of reality television increasingly defines the political arena: what we're seeing is real, but it's also being put on for show.

And of course, reality television is how Donald Trump became a truly household name. He has long been at home in the genre, while the rest of us are only getting used to it. Rather than being shaped by the contours of the presidency and using it to advance an agenda, he has tended to embrace it as a platform for a kind of reality-television act. His ambition has been directed at making himself the most visible player in the drama of our culture war, filling a great deal of space in our national consciousness but leaving a void in our constitutional system.

ON THE WHOLE, THE THIRD BRANCH OF OUR FEDERAL GOVERN-ment—the judiciary—has done a little better at resisting these trends in recent decades. That's not to say that it has been immune to them, of course. At this point, a significant portion of the problem that has traditionally been described as judicial activism is actually a form of this broader transformation of institutions from molds to platforms: some judges have come to think of the bench as a stage and of their work as part of a moralistic melodrama. Especially in recent years, such activism has tended to involve not so much the extension of judicial authorities or the imposition of a particular theory of constitutional interpretation as moralistic performance art geared to the culture war.

On some of the hottest cultural controversies (almost all of which reach the courts sooner or later) judges have found it difficult to resist grandstanding. This happens in decisions from the Right and from the Left, in judicial-philosophy terms, and sometimes even in decisions that reflect a kind of originalist jurisprudence but are still wrapped up in theatrics.[10]

Broadly speaking, however, the federal courts have been much more resistant to these trends than our other governing institutions. They have kept some sanctums for themselves, some rooms where deliberation is possible. They have staunchly resisted televising most oral arguments, for instance, and have retained the fundamentally textual character of judicial communication with the broader public. Their efforts on this front help show that there can be gradations of transparency even in the work of public institutions. An oral argument is not a private deliberation, but neither is it a television show.

And although the courts (and the legal profession, its schools, and other institutions, as we will see) have without question been somewhat politicized and turned into arenas of combat in our pervasive culture war, they have still done a better job than many other governing institutions in appealing to an ideal of integrity that is fundamentally institutional in character and also rooted in something of a professional ethos. There are exceptional cases, regarding exceptional issues, in which judges do become cultural partisans and actors. But in most of their day-to-day work, they are still recognizably distinct and formed by their institutional roles. As such, public trust in the courts has tended to remain higher than in the other institutions of our national politics.

It is tempting to assume that the courts have been a little more resistant to these pressures because the judiciary is less democratic than the Congress or the presidency. As the courts are less subject to direct electoral pressure and less answerable to political activists and voters, they might be better able to keep some distance from the populist tenor of our time, and to resist the pressure for total transparency. There is certainly some truth to that, but the story is not nearly so simple. We can get a sense of its complexity by considering the transformation of what are (at least in formal terms) among the least democratic of our political institutions yet the most thoroughly overtaken by the institutional evolution we have been tracing: the political parties.

OUR TWO MAJOR PARTIES ARE NOT CONSTITUTIONAL INSTITUTIONS, of course. But in different forms and under different names, two distinct parties have been part of our politics almost from the very beginning. There is no way to organize a representative democracy like ours without political parties, and the particular rules of the game in our system practically guarantee that two big parties will divide up nearly all the elected offices between them.[11]

But that they are the means by which we organize electioneering and structure some of the work of governance does not make the parties democratic institutions. In fact, the parties are private, not public. They are civic organizations, answerable to their members and capable of setting rules on their own terms. Their work is constrained by some legal boundaries on campaign spending and coordination, but it is ultimately shaped far more by private decisions made by the members, candidates, officeholders, officers, and staffers who compose the party. Rather than instruments of popular democratic action, the parties are in essence depositories of political professionalism.

The parties therefore act as channels for partisanship: they direct and guide it, they give it shape and form with the aim of enabling electoral success and effective governance in accordance with some internally agreed-upon views or goals. The role of the parties in the accelerating polarization we now live with is therefore not what we might first imagine. Growing partisanship is a sign of weaker parties, not stronger ones. The purpose of a party is to embody a political vision and enable a broad coalition to cohere around it. That means the parties have strong institutional incentives to moderate their own extremes and to make their pitches as broadly appealing as possible. They want to win different kinds of voters in different kinds of places. Thus, they are naturally inclined to seek common denominators and not to emphasize intensely divisive positions. They need to persuade and win converts, not just rev up committed loyalists.

Parties do this particularly by controlling whom their candidates will be and what kinds of messages they will convey. And this process—choosing on behalf of the party who will represent it and how—is itself almost inherently undemocratic. It involves people on the inside making choices that narrow the options available to the wider body of voters. As political scientist E. E. Schattschneider famously put it, "Democracy is to be found between the parties, not within them." The parties are not associations of the people who vote for them but small organizations of professional and nearly professional activists. It would be impossible for the tens of millions of people who vote for each party's candidates to genuinely participate in the life of an institution together. But that does not mean that the party is not responsive to the needs of those voters. "The parties do not need laws to make them sensitive to the wishes of the voters any more than we need laws compelling merchants to please their customers," Schattschneider concluded. "The sovereignty of the voter consists in his freedom of choice."[12]

This is, of course, a fundamentally elitist way of understanding the role and character of a political party. It suggests that the party consists of a small minority of people working within an institution to frame the options for the broader citizenry in the electoral process. This picture of American democracy did not sit well with many activists, particularly in the Democratic Party, during the second half of the twentieth century. The same post-Watergate wave of populism and reform that brought transparency to Congress also brought far greater democratization to the political parties. Through binding primaries and similar mechanisms (rather than party conventions), beginning in the 1970s the choice of candidates up and down the ballot was taken away from party elders, elected officials, and political professionals and given to the millions of voters who compose the party's electorate. The Democrats started this process, but the Republicans soon followed suit.

Even this was not enough for many activists, however, and some states adopted the practice of open primaries, which allow even people who are not formally members of a political party to vote in that party's primary, provided only that they don't also vote in the other party's primary. This made the process of candidate selection a kind of pre-election open to the broader public rather than a deliberative process within a private institution. At the same time, over the course of the latter decades of the twentieth century and the beginning of our own, reforms of the campaign-finance system sharply constrained the resources available to parties and instead drove political money toward smaller, outside groups of activists. These changes were intended to encourage participation and transparency—to weaken elites and empower the broader public. But their effects have been to transform the parties from molds of political conflict into platforms for political conflict. The difference has turned out to be immense.

In effect, the parties lost some crucial elements of their inner lives. Rather than allowing political professionals and dedicated volunteers to engage in the work of crafting broad coalitions, the modern party is an open forum for individual candidates, which means that those candidates best suited to acting on a platform on their own have an edge. The result of this is that parties have become deprofessionalized, cannot control their own internal processes, and are increasingly exposed to the power and pressure of political-celebrity culture. This increasingly unmolded political culture then sets raw partisanship loose upon society.

In the 2016 presidential election, for instance, both parties saw genuine outsiders—candidates who had not even been members of the party in the very recent past—pursue their presidential nominations. The Democratic Party was barely able to hold back such a challenge from Vermont senator Bernie Sanders, and the Republican Party handed its nomination to Donald Trump. In both cases, most party elites wanted badly to resist the incursion, but found themselves in a situation in which it seemed almost illegitimate for the party to insist on its prerogatives as an institution—leaving it instead to accept its altered role as an open platform for democratic expression.

Such weak parties easily fall prey to individual politicians building their private brands and appealing to our desire for authenticity. This is an appeal rooted in a reaction to the politics of the 1960s and early '70s, inclined toward broad and unmediated representation and against elite power. But the case for direct participation has been so thoroughly triumphant that we now lean much too far in that direction—and away from mediating political institutions. It is time to shift the weight back some. Our politics does need a significant degree of citizen participation, and its institutions must be responsive to voter pressures. But the parties must also be formative of voter pressure and of a healthier partisanship rooted in institutional commitments that point toward public spiritedness.

Ironically, then, partisanship is running rampant because our parties are not strong enough. Reformers looking to moderate that partisanship should find ways of encouraging the parties to act as institutions again. For instance, reforming campaign-finance laws so that the parties, rather than political action committees, are the organizations doing the bulk of the fundraising and spending would help incentivize candidates to broaden rather than narrow their appeals and would move the parties to select their candidates accordingly. Reintroducing some layers of political professionalism into the candidate-selection process (for example, by allowing a party's elected officials to have more of a role in screening potential candidates at the outset) would also be of use.[13]

THE PURPOSE OF SUCH REFORMS WOULD BE TO REVIVE THE PARTIES as functional, formative institutions. The same goal should motivate reformers of our other political institutions. The absence of self-confidently formative institutions—their replacement by mere platforms for celebrity entertainers and culture-war virtue signaling—has been at the center of a decay of our system of government and a decline in the public's respect and regard for it.

To contemplate that decay and decline is to grasp that the problem with our politics today is not fundamentally a problem of ideology but of social psychology. We aren't exactly disagreeing about public policy, because we aren't really talking about public policy much, except to the degree that various general categories of policy ideas (like "a tax cut" or "single payer") serve as totems for tribal affiliations. Rather, the dysfunctions of our political culture at this point are the result of a kind of breakdown of our political psychology, unleashed and unmoored from institutional constraints. This is in no small part because many of the elites who shape our political culture have allowed themselves to be plucked out of the various institutions that normally refine and elevate the work they do and to be plopped instead as individuals, unconstrained and unprotected, onto essentially performative stages—deforming our politics into the contours of the broader culture war. The solutions to such a problem cannot be ideological. Well-intentioned projects to seek a moderate middle or to help people of different views hear each other aren't likely to succeed on their own. There's even reason to think that just hearing people we disagree with more often could drive us further apart, absent other changes.[14]

This is because context matters. It matters how we encounter one another, and what the structures of our interactions and accommodations look like. Those structures are established in the forms of our institutions. So a revival of our political culture requires us to focus not just on ideology but also on institutions—their internal cultures, and their capacity to forge integrity. Our social psychology can only really be reformed and repaired within institutions. And that means that part of the solution to the frenzy of contemporary partisanship needs to come from partisans of our institutions.

In the formal and informal structures of our constitutional system, the deformations rooted in an increasingly theatrical approach to governing have not only made our institutions less focused on their constitutional purposes but also made them all more like one another. They have all come to be engaged in the same melodramatic enterprise, competing with each other on that field, rather than on the field set out for their competitive and cooperative engagement. In the process, all the institutions involved lose their distinct characters, their distinct purposes, their distinct forms of ambition, and their distinct modes of integrity. This blurring of boundaries is a problem we will trace well beyond the political sphere.

Indeed, while the dangers of this shift in the way we understand institutions may be particularly easy to see with regard to our political institutions, what we find in politics is just one instance of a larger pattern. The trouble is much more widespread. And it becomes particularly acute where integrity is most essential. Considering this facet of the problem can take us deeper toward an understanding of the challenge our society confronts.

four

PROFESSIONAL HELP

S OME INSTITUTIONS DERIVE THEIR VERY PURPOSE AND SIGNIF-
icance from their commitment to deliver integrity in the work
of the people within them. This is particularly true of the professions as institutions: the lawyer, the doctor, the nurse, the teacher,
and the scientist are people we regard with respect because the work
they do is guided by institutional patterns and boundaries, and because they are formed accordingly. To be such a professional is not
only to have a certain job but almost to become a certain type of
human being.

What we call "the professions" are distinct from other occupations precisely because they are somewhat institutionalized, in just
the sense that we have been tracing. They are characterized by some
combination of formal training (often through professional schools
or certifications), a set of institutional structures of which the profession is the guardian (like courts, hospitals, schools, churches, or
labs), specialized knowledge, some degree of self-regulation, and an
important social purpose that the profession exists to serve—which

tends to yield a strong internal ethos among practitioners. In uncertain situations, a professional asks himself, "What should I do here, given my professional responsibilities?" And his profession will generally have an answer to that question.[1]

The professions are distinct from the organizations they operate, like the corporation in which a professional might work. In fact, professionals help us see more clearly the distinction between institutions and organizations. The professional code can act as a crucial source of protection against corporate abuses by holding some ideal above organizational affiliation and power. A professional might call out corruption in his company or school or clinic precisely in the name of a professional code.

Moreover, a profession is not just a collection of people with a certain body of knowledge and skills. It's a collection of people using their knowledge and skills to achieve a morally freighted purpose, and doing so in a way constrained by obligations and responsibilities. It is a form of organizing knowledge, people, and action toward a particular way of working in the world.

In this respect, we might say that the professions are especially adept at building social capital. They give their members skills, norms, and habits; they provide them with networks and frameworks. They also offer objects for devotion and commitment—by inspiring loyalty both to the proper practice of a discipline and to fellow practitioners of it. The professions are depositories of expertise and framers of its proper uses. They give people a part to play in a larger whole.

But this also means that the decline in public confidence in institutions in recent decades has involved a decline in public confidence in many professions, and therefore also in the authority of expertise in general. Because they tend to ensconce their members in formative institutional structures, the professions are almost inherently elitist and are naturally at home among society's establishments. The democratization and fragmentation of knowledge in our time have meant that the specialized knowledge once held in trust by professionals is now often widely available outside the boundaries of the professions. The institutional structures built to develop, filter, assess, and convey that knowledge, then, are challenged by outside competitors who may not be subject to the same constraints as the professionals. In one field after another, this has put pressure on professionals to step outside the bounds of their professions and play a different role.

Examples of how this has played out could easily be drawn from law, the sciences, medicine, teaching, accounting, and many other professions. But, given our emphasis on the changing place of institutions in American life in this era of culture war, and given that we began in the last chapter with government and politics, the state of contemporary journalism might offer a particularly helpful illustration.

Journalism has not always been understood as a formal profession, but in the course of the twentieth century it went through a transformation that left it with all the characteristics of one, and with links and similarities to many other core professions. Like those other professions, journalism in our day confronts a crisis.

JOURNALISM IS NOT IN CRISIS IN EVERY RESPECT, OF COURSE. DEMAND for its offerings is strong, as public interest in current events, and politics in particular, has soared in this era of political turbulence. The supply of journalism is plentiful too, and its quality—while obviously variable—is surely on par with any golden age of reporting we might point to. The economics of journalism in the information age has been brutal, but some journalistic outfits large and small have gradually been finding effective ways to deal with it. The freedom of the press, which has not always been secure in our country, is in no real jeopardy now, or even in much question or dispute.

So what's the problem? The crisis now confronting American journalism is a crisis of public confidence—a crisis of integrity and trust. President Trump has frequently given vent to the attitudes underlying this loss of trust. "The Fake News Media has never been so wrong or so dirty. Purposely incorrect stories and phony sources to meet their agenda of hate. Sad!" So Trump wrote on Twitter on June 13, 2017. This was a thoroughly characteristic statement of his regarding the press—unusual neither in tone nor in substance. That the president of the United States would speak about the profession like this and that he would do so on a social media platform that affords him direct access to many millions of Americans on his own terms are marks of the peculiar situation of journalism, and especially political journalism, in contemporary American life.[2]

The trouble, moreover, is not so much about trust in individual journalists, or even about trust in particular publications, networks, or platforms—though some come in for more criticism than others. Rather, it is a matter of trust in American journalism as a whole, or at least trust in so-called mainstream journalism as an institution, understood as part of the array of institutions that compose the American establishment.

American journalists have never been at ease understanding their work as part of such an array of institutions. Journalism in a democracy always prides itself on its ability to hone a certain civic skepticism, to hold leaders to account, to uncover important facts hidden from the public, and to enable citizens to assess government officials. In this sense, American journalism sometimes imagines itself to be countercultural or an antiestablishment force like the muckrakers of old. There are, of course, elements of this way of thinking and operating in the work of contemporary journalism. But journalism in America underwent a multi-decade process of institutionalization, over the first half or so of the twentieth century, that fundamentally transformed its character.

By the latter decades of that century, political journalism had largely come to be practiced by highly educated cultural elites in America's major cities, and many of the most prominent media enterprises came to be owned by large corporations or the very wealthy. Journalists fell into the habit of applying their skepticism mostly toward critics of elite institutions and challengers to elite norms, and their work had come to be implicitly protective of what might be called an establishmentarian status quo. Yet most political journalists never came to conceive of themselves and their work in this way and so were not prepared to defend themselves against a rising tide of anti-institutional sentiment.

That tide has continued to rise in this century. American journalism, like most of our major institutions, has been subject to intense social, cultural, and economic pressures that have undone some of its institutional forms and character—undermining its ethic and its social standing and increasingly subjecting it to competition from a range of upstarts. America's media giants are still largely populated by highly educated elites and largely owned by major corporations or extremely wealthy individuals, but they are now engaged in a struggle for dominance with less-established competitors of various types. No one imagines that the major newspapers or television networks have some inherent claim on our trust or attention.

In this sense, American journalism offers an instance of a larger pattern in our national life, as public trust in nearly every profession has plummeted in recent decades while the culture has grown far more variegated, fragmented, and diverse. But the crisis of American journalism is especially acute because journalism conveys information that is only valuable to the degree it is deemed reliable, so a crisis of confidence presents it with a distinctly challenging problem.

This is by no means the first time that American journalism has found itself facing a crisis of confidence. Each past crisis, like the current one, has reflected the distinct cultural characteristics of its era. Considering some of those could help us distinguish and better understand today's particular circumstances.

One notable crisis of journalism offers a sharp contrast to today's situation. In 1942, with the world at war and the nation having already endured a decade of nearly uninterrupted emergency mobilizations of various sorts, a number of prominent Americans began to feel that the freedom of the press was threatened. Henry Luce, the publisher of *Time* magazine, approached University of Chicago president Robert M. Hutchins about launching an inquiry into the state of that essential liberty. Hutchins gathered a commission of eminent scholars and took up the question over a period of several years. The result, known as the Hutchins Commission report, was published at the end of 1946 and offers a snapshot of the state of the press at mid-century.[3]

While the commission was charged with contemplating the state of the freedom of the press, it did direct itself to the question of public trust in journalism. There were reasons for worry on that front, in the opinion of the commission's members, because of the process of intense and rapid consolidation that American journalism was undergoing. "The modern press itself is a new phenomenon," the commission noted.

> Its typical unit is the great agency of mass communication. These agencies can facilitate thought and discussion. They can stifle it. They can advance the progress of civilization or they can thwart it. They can debase and vulgarize mankind. They can endanger the peace of the world; they can do so accidentally, in a fit of absence of mind. They can play up or down the news and its significance, foster and feed emotions, create complacent fictions and blind spots, misuse the great words, and uphold empty slogans. Their scope and power are increasing every day as new instruments become available to them. These instruments can spread

lies faster and farther than our forefathers dreamed when they enshrined the freedom of the press in the First Amendment to our Constitution.[4]

In some respects, these are concerns very similar to those we might hear today. The power of the press is enormous, and its capacity to abuse that power is therefore very great. These are worries about the concentration of power and about who wields it. In a sense, therefore, they are inherently populist worries, despite the distinctly elite character of the Hutchins Commission and its members. They are worries about what we have been calling insiderism—the abuse of power by the denizens of a powerful institution. Arguments like these are still the ones most commonly voiced by today's populist critics of the mainstream media.

And yet, the way the Hutchins Commission thought about that concentration of power can help us see just how much things have changed. "A technical society requires concentration of economic power," the commission argued.

Since such concentration is a threat to democracy, democracy replies by breaking up some centers of power that are too large and too strong and by controlling, or even owning, others. Modern society requires great agencies of mass communication. They, too, are concentrations of power. But breaking up a vast network of communication is a different thing from breaking up an oil monopoly or a tobacco monopoly. If the people set out to break up a unit of communication on the theory that it is too large and strong, they may destroy a service which they require. Moreover, since action to break up an agency of communication must be taken at the instance of a department of the government, the risk is considerable that the freedom of the press will be imperiled through the application of political pressure by that department.[5]

It seemed obvious to the commission's members that a modern society would require centralized media, and that there was little hope of breaking up such a concentration. This is not nearly so obvious now. In fact, the commission's stark terms might compel an observer of the contemporary media environment to wonder if the problem we confront should actually be understood as a problem of concentration at all.

There are certainly some significant concentrations of power in some facets of the media, as there are throughout our economy. It's true that a few large corporations control the means by which vast swaths of our society obtain their information. But the most significant of these are not actually media companies, in the sense that they do not produce journalistic content; they are information-management and social media companies, such as Google, Facebook, and Twitter. They possess the ability to filter our information through complex algorithms that can exercise enormous influence over what reaches us and under what circumstances.

We will consider these still-novel centers of power in chapter 6. But although public concerns about them are growing, these are not the foremost targets of populist anger toward journalism. That anger is directed toward the power of the traditional media, which has actually been declining and fragmenting for decades—lately with the help of those very social media platforms. Long gone are the days when network evening newscasts would draw the eyes of an absolute majority of the nation, or when two or three major newspapers monopolized the public's understanding of key national events.

Complaints about the media still naturally fall into the terms and tones of popular rejection of elite authority, but (as President Trump's tweet above suggests) they often have at least as much to do with skepticism about the integrity of the mainstream media as with its power. Indeed, far from a function of concentration, this skepticism seems rooted at least partially in a breakdown of confidence that has to do with the multiplicity and fragmentation of sources of information. It is not so much the media's power, or the power of its owners, that makes it hard to trust as it is its lack of evident reliability and integrity.

In this regard, today's media crisis looks more like some challenges that American journalism has confronted at times of fragmentation and fracture, rather than in the peculiar era of consolidation in the middle of the twentieth century. Perhaps above all, the media landscape now resembles the circumstances of journalism in the early republic—when barriers to entry were relatively low and the media environment was teeming with mostly small voices.

One telling artifact of that era is a brief essay published anonymously by Benjamin Franklin in 1789 called "An Account of the Supremest Court of Judicature in Pennsylvania, viz., The Court of the Press." Like much of Franklin's writing, this short essay is at least partially satirical. But it advances a very serious point: that anyone with access to a printing press can make wild, unfounded accusations and destroy the reputation of anyone he might choose to target.

The press has great power with no clear limits on its use, Franklin worried. It is in this sense like a court without law. "It may receive and promulgate accusations of all kinds against all persons and characters among the citizens of the State, and even against all inferior courts," he wrote, "and may judge, sentence, and condemn to infamy, not only private individuals, but public bodies, etc., with or without inquiry or hearing, at the court's direction." This court, Franklin noted, is not governed by any clear rules:

> The accused is allowed no grand jury to judge of the truth of the accusation before it is publicly made, nor is the name of the accuser made known to him, nor has he an opportunity of confronting the witnesses against him, for they are kept in the dark as in the Spanish court of Inquisition. Nor is there any petty jury

of his peers, sworn to try the truth of the charges. The proceedings are also sometimes so rapid that an honest, good citizen may find himself suddenly and unexpectedly accused, and in the same morning judged and condemned and sentence pronounced against him, that he is a rogue and a villain. Yet, if an officer of this court receives the slightest check for misconduct in this his office, he claims immediately the rights of a free citizen by the constitution and demands to know his accuser, to confront the witnesses, and to have a fair trial by a jury of his peers.[6]

The danger of this pseudo court abusing its power is thus immense, Franklin suggested. The press has the power to purvey lies—fake news, we might say—or (to recall President Trump's terms above) to spread "purposely incorrect stories and phony sources to meet their agenda of hate."

At the core of this complaint is the assertion of an absence of standards. As Franklin understood, this was a function not of the concentration of media power but precisely of its dilution. The power of the press in his time, Franklin wrote, was available to anyone who, "by education or practice in scribbling, has acquired a tolerable style as to grammar and construction, so as to bear printing; or who is possessed by a press and a few types." Anyone could become a menace in the court of public opinion, and his victims would have little recourse. "For if you make the least complaint of the judge's conduct," Franklin wrote, "he daubs his blacking balls in your face wherever he meets you; and, besides tearing your private character to flitters, marks you out for the odium of the public, as an enemy to the liberty of the press."[7]

To Franklin, there seemed no real remedy to this problem except placing constraints upon that liberty of the press. "If by the liberty of the press were understood merely the liberty of discussing the propriety of public measures and political opinions, let us have as much of it as you please," he wrote. "But if it means the liberty of affronting, calumniating, and defaming one another, I, for my part, own myself willing to part with my share of it whenever our legislators shall please so to alter the law, and shall cheerfully consent to exchange my liberty of abusing others for the privilege of not being abused myself."[8]

That remedy has, with good reason, generally been ruled out of bounds in our politics, at least beyond very narrowly constructed libel laws. Franklin wrote just over a year before the Bill of Rights was ratified, but he was well aware of the abiding commitment to the freedom of the press in American public life—a cause he had championed himself at times. He seems to have intended to raise the question of how the power of journalism to abuse its subjects might be contained rather than to seriously propose legislative limits on the press.[9]

FOR US, FRANKLIN'S COMPLAINT CAN HELP TO CLARIFY THE NATURE of a problem that today's populist hostility toward the press mostly obscures. Although critics of the press today use populist language about the power of the establishment, they seem really to be complaining about an absence of standards and integrity. They are lamenting something we are missing, not something we have too much of. They are asking, in a sense, for a more reliable and perhaps even more authoritative press.

In fact, the same might be said, up to a point, about the complaints of today's populists more generally. Although their instinctive parlance is the vocabulary of downtrodden masses crying out against the abuses of an oppressive elite, they frequently accuse that elite of being too weak, not too strong. This is surely true of Trump's populism, which treats America's core institutions as pathetic and inept, not as confident and domineering. It is a populism yearning for a lost American greatness that was made possible by a very confident establishment, even if it would also clearly be uncomfortable with some of the practices and views of that establishment.

If the essential problem is integrity, then it might be useful to consider how the press avoided the implications of Franklin's argument and how its reputation might have come to be reinforced at different times without putting an end to its freedom. This is, needless to say, a subject ripe with complexity and suitable for a multivolume work, not a brief chapter. It has also received no shortage of scholarly attention over the years. But here I will gesture toward one facet of the question that seems particularly relevant to our contemporary circumstances: the emergence of professional journalism as an institution in American life, which involved both the consolidation of journalism as an industry and the professionalization of journalism as a practice.

The arc of that process followed the path of a broader consolidation of American life, from the middle decades of the nineteenth century through the middle of the twentieth, driven by technological advances, economic transformation, and political reforms. Under the pressure of industrialization, the influence of progressive politics, and the emergence of genuinely mass media, the scale of American life increased dramatically and drove a consolidation of politics, economics, culture, and national identity. One result was the emergence of national newspapers—and later also radio and television—which gradually spurred the development of a standardized, formalized journalism very different from the sort Franklin had described.[10]

Barriers to entry, particularly barriers of cost and technological complexity, meant that journalism was no longer accessible to anyone who could write clearly or print pamphlets. It was instead the purview of large, organized corporate entities that insisted on some degree of formal structure. Journalism gradually became a profession—with some broadly accepted general standards, means of training new professionals (as journalism schools popped up throughout the country), and a strong ethic and straightforward set of common commitments.

This was no panacea to the trouble with journalistic power, of course. Indeed, it yielded the institutionalized, centralized journalism about which the Hutchins Commission raised concerns. But by becoming more formalized, the profession was at least offering a response to some concerns about basic integrity, and it became better able to lay claim to public confidence and trust.

That response took a form similar to (and plainly modeled on) scientific integrity, proposing an institutionalized commitment to a process of verification that aimed to distinguish fact from fiction. This, in turn, allowed for the development of a journalistic code of ethics, layers of something like peer review in the editorial process, and procedures for punishing, shaming, or ostracizing violators. As with the scientific method, this procedure made it possible for professionals within journalism to take pride in their humility—that is, to see as a strength the fact that they would only assert what they could reasonably prove. That ethic required both serious professional discipline and institutions capable of prioritizing professional standards over personal glory or political victory. To make people proud to be humble demands an institution with a firm sense of purpose and real self-respect.[11]

In journalism as in science, this idealized form of the standard of verification could never be fully realized in practice. But the ideal has long exercised a powerful influence on the way journalists see themselves and their work, and it helped make possible some genuine public trust in the institutions of American journalism.

This consolidated form of American journalism reached its apex in the middle decades of the last century, peaking around the mid-1970s. In that era, public confidence in journalism rose to extraordinary heights, following a broader trend of solid trust in America's large institutions. In 1976, Gallup found that 72 percent of Americans had confidence in the news media—the highest level they have found in nearly seven decades of polling. Since that time, trust in journalism has plummeted. In 2018, Gallup found that only 32 percent of the public expressed trust in the press. At the same time, journalism, like some other key institutions, has gone through an intense process of deconsolidation. Traditional, formal journalistic institutions have grown fewer (and more concentrated), but nontraditional and informal sources of information have sprouted up everywhere—and have applied intense pressures on traditional journalism. As barriers to entry have fallen dramatically thanks to technology, and as public expectations have shifted, today's journalistic landscape looks more and more like that of Franklin's time, with its attendant strengths and weaknesses.[12]

The fact that the degree to which the public has lost faith in the media is on par with the loss of faith in other key institutions suggests there may be no way to counteract this trend without reversing a far larger set of social forces. Yet journalism is different because, as noted above, trust is its currency in a more fundamental sense. It exists to convey information and cannot perform its basic function if it does not have the trust of its audience. Journalism is also uniquely subject to the effects of some important technological innovations in recent years, especially the rise of social media.

In fact, it is the internet and social media, perhaps more than anything else, that have helped transform American journalism in this century—and that account for the fact that this transformation looks very much like a change from a mold institution to a platform institution. By multiplying and fragmenting sources of information, the web and social media have turned the work of journalism into a means of self-expression for different groups of Americans. People filter and select among news sources and then distribute the work of those they prefer (or those chosen for them by algorithms meant to predict their preferences) among their virtual circles. By providing powerful independent platforms for dissemination, social media in particular has turned many journalists from participants in the work of institutions into managers of their own personal images. Even reporters for major national newspapers and television networks—whose formal work is subject to layers of editing and verification—now have a constant presence on Twitter and other social media platforms, offering up both reporting and commentary on an ongoing basis. This makes it hard to distinguish the work of individuals from the work of institutions and increasingly turns journalistic institutions into platforms for the personal brands of individual journalists.

Those brands, moreover, often plainly fall on clearly distinguishable sides of our culture wars (very frequently on the Left), and journalists promoting a politicized self-image outside the professional, institutional framework of journalism cannot help but undermine the integrity of the profession. At the same time, the elite journalistic institutions themselves increasingly lean into the culture war. They do this both in search of audience share and under the influence of a younger generation of journalists who have been shaped by other platform institutions (particularly elite universities, as we will see) to expect the institutions they are part of to openly affirm and display their cultural attitudes and political instincts.

Many older professional journalists now have stories to tell about clashes between this younger, more activist journalistic ethic and the traditional professionalism of the newsroom. In April 2018, Joe Pompeo of *Vanity Fair* pulled back the veil on this dynamic at the *New York Times*. "For most of its history, the *Times* has been an autocracy, with a church-like reverence for its values and traditions," he wrote.

Rebellion, as against executive editor Howell Raines in 2003, has often been to restore the old order rather than to overthrow it.

But, as at many newsrooms and media offices, and in the culture at large, this is a moment of generational conflict not seen since the 1960s. "I've been feeling a lot lately like the newsroom is split into roughly the old-guard category, and the young and 'woke' category, and it's easy to feel that the former group doesn't take into account how much the future of the paper is predicated on the talent contained in the latter one," a *Times* employee in that latter group told me a couple months ago.

The nature of the divide in expectations falls precisely into the pattern we have been tracing here. As an older *Times* veteran put it to Pompeo, "I think a lot of this younger generation were brought up to believe that it's very important that their voices be heard, and so I think it's a bit harder to fit into an institution where it's less than democratic in some ways. One generation came of age where they entered this esteemed institution and tried to find a way to fit into it, and this other generation has an expectation that the institution will change to accommodate them. That's the essence of the tension."[13]

This describes a tension between the mold and platform understandings of core institutions. Or rather, it describes a party of the institution fighting a party of the culture war for control of some of the commanding heights of journalism. The struggle plays out in the semipublic spaces of social media in ways that weaken and muddle the distinctions between professional and amateur work, private and public views, journalism and politics.

These trends feed into a cycle that exacerbates mistrust, undermines standards, makes comparisons of reliability challenging, and leaves the public understandably skeptical about the integrity of contemporary journalism. It also contributes to more traditional institutional failures—failures to enforce journalistic standards, resist various political hysterias, and appropriately restrain the power of the press—that further contribute to public cynicism about journalism.

There can be no simple solution to this problem. But a proper diagnosis must be the first step toward even partial remedies, and thinking institutionally can help us cut through the fog of contemporary populist rhetoric and seek a clearer understanding of the problem. By thinking about the crisis of journalism in institutional terms, we can begin to see a few paths that American journalism might chart to at least modestly improve its standing.

First, journalists should see that the problem their profession now confronts is a function of public doubts about the integrity of their work. The freedom of the press is not under any genuine threat, and they are not really the victims of a wave of abject relativism sweeping the nation and causing some Americans to deny the existence of empirical reality. Rather, they are working in an environment that makes it difficult for the public to trust their work, and their own practices frequently contribute to this environment. This is the problem they should seek to solve. That should make demonstrated integrity a valuable source of comparative advantage, which means in turn that the value of certain formal, institutional structures—a code of conduct taken seriously, an overt professionalism, a system of vetting and fact-checking, a newsroom, an editorial team—should not be underestimated.

Second, they should see that journalistic institutions are valued not only for the work they produce but for the ethic they engender. This means, among other things, that journalists should be particularly careful to avoid the culture of individual celebrity in American life, which is the very opposite of the culture of institutional integrity. Too often now, prominent political reporters in particular can be found engaged in a never-ending, loose, unstructured form of conversational commentary on television, on Twitter, and elsewhere—a conversation carried on in public view but outside the procedural and ethical boundaries of their workplaces, which makes it increasingly difficult for journalism to lay claim to institutional integrity and nearly impossible for journalists to avoid petty partisanship. Journalists inclined to complain about how Donald Trump has behaved in office should consider whether President Trump's behavior relative to what the presidency is might be unnervingly similar to the behavior of leading political reporters relative to what journalism is. Both are playing out a self-indulgent celebrity version of the real thing, and in both cases this renders them less able to perform their appropriate and essential work.

Third, journalists should recognize that their profession may have a particularly important role to play in any recovery of confidence in American institutions. This is, for one thing, because journalism stands to offer a means to channel our mistrust of other institutions, and so to keep our skepticism from curdling into cynicism. The self-image of American journalists as valiant muckrakers speaking truth to power is of course frequently exaggerated. Most journalists are highly educated cultural elites—and much of what they do implicitly involves defending the preconceptions of the powerful, which they generally share. But journalistic institutions that responsibly uncover abuses of power can nonetheless play a vital role in discouraging the larger society from imagining the worst about its major institutions in every realm of life. Holding leaders to account can ultimately reinforce public confidence.

To be trusted as a source of information, however, the profession must better secure itself against the charge of partisanship. Achieving that, in this arena as in others we are considering, will require a strong party of the profession within the various institutions of American journalism, calling for restraint and helping journalists see the reasons for abstaining from the culture war. The only way to really make that possible would be through a reinvigoration of institutional channels of status, acclaim, belonging, and formation. It would require journalists to understand themselves as insiders bound by a common code of conduct and answerable to each other and to a larger public. That would take a conscious effort, which would need to begin from a recognition of the problem.

THE SAME IS TRUE AT THIS POINT FOR MANY OF THE OTHER PROFES-sions that have been losing public trust and esteem. Each is distinct, and each relates to our increasingly bitter and divisive culture war in different ways. But each has traveled this path.

In the legal profession, for instance, the pattern is plainly evident: elite law schools in particular have increasingly been transformed into battlegrounds in the culture war, and the profession has been gradually shorn of its strong, confident, formative identity. Lawyers have a distinct place in our particular social order—as interpreters of the legal frameworks of democratic life, as careful reformers of those frameworks, and as agents of fellow citizens in need of pru-dent counsel. A professional code that accustoms even the most elite lawyers to serve as agents of others and that holds them to a standard that has more to do with integrity than with raw intellect would be one useful way to help humble them and to legitimate their standing and their privileges. That kind of professional ethic is by no means gone altogether, but particularly in its elite precincts (as with journal-ism) the legal profession is increasingly unrestrained by it.[14]

The pattern is not nearly so clear in, say, medicine, where the pro-fession's core purpose is inherently more insulated from culture-war pressures. But the general direction of medicine's professional evo-lution—its loss of control over privileged knowledge, challenges to its expertise, and abuses of its authority—is not so different. Other professions fall in different places along this continuum, but the arc of their evolution bears some similarities to that of journalism: elite consolidation in the middle of the last century led to concerns about insiderism and the abuse of power but was then followed by a period of de-professionalization, competition from amateurs, a re-duced information advantage, lower barriers to entry, and in time a surrender to fragmentation and the pressures of celebrity culture, leading to concerns about outsiderism and irresponsibility.

This is the arc of many of our other public and private institutions too, as we have seen. It is a function of a fragmenting society and economy, but at its core is a changing set of attitudes and expecta-tions about institutions. For the professions, the effect of this gradual transformation has been disastrous. A profession offers its members an essential service: It restrains and protects them, it gives them pur-pose and belonging, and it provides them with a valued place in a larger social order. Denied this service, professionals are isolated and left exposed to perform, and to be drawn into the gaping maw of the culture war.

For our larger society, the consequences are hardly less dire. We need trustworthy expertise and professionalism. If we cannot rely on professionals at key moments, we cannot hope to build up social trust or to address core social problems. And we run the particular risk of losing access to a common ground of facts and premises that might serve as a foundation for our private judgments and our public life. The professions exist in large part to handle knowledge responsi-bly. So when we cannot trust them, we incline to be irresponsible in how we handle knowledge.

Grasping the importance of protecting social forms shaped for seeking the truth and handling knowledge with integrity can take us one more step toward the heart of the social crisis we face—and toward the heart of the culture war too.

five

CAMPUS CULTURES

A MERICAN HIGHER EDUCATION IS A WONDER OF THE WORLD. We are privileged to be home to an exceptional concentration of the greatest universities on earth, which serve as magnets for talent, fountains of dynamism, and living links to the roots of our civilization. The university in the West is a medieval institution, still shaped by forms and traditions that date back to long before the history of our own nation. But the university has also always had a special place in the American imagination, and we have developed an approach to academic life that is distinctly ours—seeing the university as essential for republican citizenship, as a democratizing force, and as a means to opportunity and upward mobility.

And yet, we also have a long tradition of seeing the university as an institution in crisis. In that sense, at least, our time is not unique. Complaints about lax academic standards and lazy, pampered students are as old as the university itself—as are student protests about both campus concerns and political controversies. Anxiety about radical professors corrupting students and undermining society's morals can be found in the annals of Harvard, America's first university, as early as the first decade of the eighteenth century. Competing notions of what the fundamental purpose of the university should be roiled the American academy throughout the nineteenth century, particularly as practical-minded new land-grant universities were chartered alongside a profusion of religiously affiliated schools with distinct moral missions. The twentieth century saw not only wave after wave of intense campus radicalism but also a transformation of the academy's relationship with government, the military, and corporate America—all of which sparked heated controversies within and without the university.[1]

That there has always been a sense of unease about the state of higher education in America by no means suggests that we should downplay contemporary concerns about it, however. These past crises were real, and they were often also reflections of broader problems in American society that rose to the surface with unusual force in the university—where the American elite has sent its children and has honed its priorities and values. That means today's very real university crisis can also teach us something about the state of our country and our institutions.

In fact, in some important respects the trends we are tracing across institutions are most intensely evident, and their consequences are most acute, in the academy. The campus is where the culture war is often most fully articulated and lived out. But just for that reason, it is also where we might get beyond shallow caricatures of the sides of that conflict and think about what really drives the disputes that feed it.

IT CAN BE HARD TO DISTINGUISH NOVEL CONFLICTS FROM LONG-standing tensions in academic life because the academy is actually many things at the same time. Our society demands an awful lot of its universities. They are expected to be training grounds for future professionals, gateways to economic mobility, sanctuaries for moral and philosophical exploration, havens for basic scientific inquiry, nurseries of expertise in every field of endeavor, fonts of public spiritedness and civic learning, hothouses of political engagement, and even providers of food, housing, entertainment, and leisure—all in conditions of safety, freedom, and order.

One effect of this immense array of aims is that academic institutions in America are incredibly diverse. The academy is so diverse, in fact, that we should be careful about speaking of the university as a general category. Even if we take just the four-year degree-granting institutions of higher education in our country, we would still be looking at more than three thousand different institutions, with different goals, histories, personalities, ambitions, strengths, and weaknesses.

Pretty much every one of these universities serves numerous, competing purposes at once. The difficulty of contending with these countervailing pressures and demands has long been a defining challenge of the American academy, and so is actually one way in which it does make sense to speak of "the university," and even of a crisis of the university. Different crises of the academy in different times have often come down to imbalances among these demands.

Finding a balance can be hard because many of the objectives we want universities to pursue are in direct tension with one another. The sociologist Robert Nisbet took note of this in describing his fellow academics in 1970, in the midst of another university crisis:

> We are like a religious monastery insisting upon all the affluence of
> a freebooting capitalism; an aristocracy masochistically torment-
> ing itself with the slogans of revolutionary democracy; a commu-
> nity of pacifist contemplatives riding off in all directions at once
> to do battle with the enemy; an enclave of intellectual autonomy

privileged to remake the entire social order through permanent politics and relentless humanitarianism. We declare ourselves an intellectual elite, fully entitled to aristocratic codes of honor and tenure, and at the same time a hurly-burly of activities that even the surrounding social order seems too small to contain.[2]

The tensions between these competing demands can be a source of energy and dynamism for the academy, especially when they are kept in some rough equilibrium. But of course, each of these conceptions views itself as primary, and seeks to be the organizing principle of all academic life.

These would-be organizing principles might be sorted into roughly three understandings of the purpose of the university as an institution, all of which have been part of the American university from its earliest days and are powerful forces on campus now. The first suggests that the university exists above all to give people the skills our economy requires. This is by far the most commonly expressed expectation of higher education, especially outside the academy. The second suggests that the university exists to give students a consciousness of the moral demands of a just society. We tend to imagine this facet of American higher education is relatively new, maybe a creation of the student protest movements of the 1960s, but in fact this was an original purpose of the university in America. The third suggests that the point of the university is to expose a rising generation to the deepest and best of the wisdom of our civilization, and so to enable a search for the truth wherever it leads, without regard for economic or sociopolitical utility. This has always been a minority pursuit on most campuses, but it has also been a core purpose of the academy since Plato first applied that name to his school in Athens in the fourth century BC.

These three visions amount to three intermingled cultures within the modern university: a culture of professional development, a culture of moral activism, and a culture of liberal education. They are distinguishable, though they have always interacted and individual academics are often engaged in more than one.

The culture of professional development is generally why we think of the university as a powerful engine of social mobility and a source of marketable skills. It is what most people want out of college, and what most people get out of it. The five most common undergraduate majors in America in 2018, in descending order of popularity, were business, nursing, psychology, biology (including pre-medicine), and engineering—all of which suggest a fundamentally professional orientation among students. The ways we often think and argue about higher-education policy generally suggest the same: the question is whether students and parents get their money's worth in terms of postcollege employment and income.[3]

As that list of majors suggests, some distinct disciplines within the academy are particularly shaped by the imperatives of professional development. The natural sciences, perhaps except at the highest reaches of elite research universities (where the commitment to basic research yields a culture of its own, more akin to liberal education), are professionally oriented in this way, as of course are the expressly professional departments and programs found in schools of medicine, nursing, law, business, and the like. These academic pursuits are generally the prime attractions in the academy, even if they are not always how academics like to think of the university.

This is not a new development. Since the birth of the earliest universities in the West during the Middle Ages, these schools have existed in large part to train professionals—at first in law, medicine, and theology, but soon in many other fields—giving them the skills and the character their occupations require.[4]

Much of the structure and infrastructure of the modern university is plainly directed to this task—and in some respects it is increasingly so. One reason is that skyrocketing tuition has made students and their families more conscious of the practical returns on their investments. Another is that massive government spending on grants for research has left the American university eager to prove its economic value and utility to the larger society.

At the same time, however, the ethos and self-understanding of the modern university is frequently shaped by the culture of moral activism. Again, it is important not to overstate the novelty of contemporary circumstances. It is no exaggeration to suggest that universities in America were founded first and foremost to advance a moral mission in society—a mission that in some important respects was not so different from the one today's campus activists pursue.

Harvard and Yale, America's first two universities, were created as conservatories for Puritan orthodoxy, and to train men of religion to move the larger community to repent of its sins and seek redemption. Many of the universities that followed in their wake have put their moral ambitions and sectarian doctrines front and center too. From the very beginning, this puritanical moralistic mission was often also commingled with the cause of legitimating the moral impulses of the American elite and so of teaching a rising generation of elites to conform to the culture into which they were maturing.

This moral aim remains a driving purpose of American higher education. Now largely shorn of its religious roots, this often looks like classroom instruction and campus political activism that demand of the larger society a kind of mass repentance for some grave collective sins. The nature of the alleged transgressions reinforces the worldview of America's elite culture, which today is largely a progressive-liberal one. The content of the doctrines advanced by campus moralists has changed a lot, then. But the motivations of the students and some of the faculty engaged in moral activism today would be quite recognizable to activists of prior ages. Some of their methods, too, and even their excesses, would not have been altogether unfamiliar to their Puritan predecessors.

Student activism has never been a foreign concept in the modern, and even the premodern, university. In his magisterial nineteenth-century history of Europe's first universities, the great British historian Hastings Rashdall noted that organized protests by students—often regarding their own living conditions or treatment but at times also about larger civic or religious matters—were common by the fourteenth century. In the United States, student activism has always been part of campus culture, and here too the causes have been a mix of parochial concerns (from poor living conditions to overbearing administrators to fear of being drafted into the military) and broader social, political, and moral concerns (from revolution in the late eighteenth century, to slavery in the nineteenth, to civil rights, war, and inequality in the twentieth and twenty-first).[5]

This culture of activism also makes its home in some particular quarters of the university and in some disciplines more than others. It is particularly prevalent as an intellectual force in the social sciences and some of the humanities. In fact, it may be fair to say that several of the social sciences are outright creatures of the culture of moral activism at this point. In his recent book *The Sacred Project of American Sociology*, for instance, Christian Smith suggests that modern sociology as an academic discipline is basically an arm of this kind of activism.[6]

But the culture of moral activism is most significant precisely as a culture. For good and ill, it pervades the communal environment of campus life in many universities, shaping the framework of praise and blame, norms and habits, expectations and peer pressure. Its intensity and the aggressiveness with which it is at times enforced are distinct features of university culture at this point and contribute to the sense that the university is becoming a monoculture, closed off to some of the traditional norms and goals of academic life.

Those norms and goals that seem most threatened are associated in particular with the third campus culture, the culture of liberal education. This is, and in America it always has been, the smallest of the campus cultures. With a few exceptions (perhaps most notably a brief liberal-arts moment in the 1950s), it has always understood itself as besieged. But it nonetheless plays a pivotal part in the life of the American academy and in enabling universities to contribute to the life of the larger society.

Liberal education is so called because it involves the kind of learning and formation required to mold free citizens. The idea reaches back to antiquity in the West, and it was long embodied in the trivium (grammar, logic, and rhetoric) and quadrivium (arithmetic, geometry, music, and astronomy) said to make up the liberal arts of the classical curriculum. The concept does more than describe certain fields, though. It constitutes a mode of learning as formation, and an approach to education that seeks the true, the good, and the beautiful.[7]

Where the culture of professional training emphasizes the practical sciences and the culture of moral activism focuses on the social sciences, liberal education in the contemporary university tends to emphasize the study of the humanities—including the arts, history, philosophy, religion, music, literature, classics, and linguistics, among others. It is, in a sense, the study of our heritage. Of course, that liberal education is focused on the humanities does not mean the humanities are focused on liberal education. But there are crucial pockets within the humanities that do see such education as their mission.

In fact, it would be fair to say that liberal education is always a matter of pockets and exceptions—and that it is countercultural to the core. One of its great twentieth-century practitioners described liberal education as "the counter-poison to mass culture." It is from that countercultural character that its value both to the student and to the larger society is often derived. It allows the individual to be exposed to higher, deeper, and more beautiful forms of knowledge than the culture of our mass democracy is likely to value. It also helps to instill in citizens judgment, character, ideals, and priorities that might counterbalance some of the excesses of democracy. This doesn't mean it necessarily forms those citizens with any particular political outlook—liberal education is neither progressive nor conservative, in the shallow political sense, and its practitioners and teachers span the ideological spectrum. But liberal education does foster an attitude that is likely to be in tension with the popular culture.[8]

Of course, these three broad campus cultures do not exhaust the multiplicity of projects, aims, and human types that populate the American academy. Some significant academic endeavors cross the boundaries between them. Perhaps most notably, the research enterprise of the natural sciences, which plays a powerful role in some American universities, embodies some elements of the culture of professional development but is also engaged in an open-ended search for knowledge. The social sciences, while often tinged with the culture of moral activism, also strive to be open to the truth, wherever it leads. Humanists are hardly unconcerned with professional certification or the career prospects of their students, and professional schools want well-rounded graduates. The point of distinguishing among the three core campus cultures is not to suggest that they are pure and unmixed types. It is only to see that they are distinct as cultures, and that the tensions and relations between them often combine to give the academic world its character.[9]

Most important, all three are *academic* cultures, in that, at their best, they do their basic work by learning and teaching. The culture of professional development aims to inculcate the knowledge, skills, habits, and character required to succeed in various fields of endeavor in American economic life—developing an ever-greater understanding of these through research and study and disseminating them by instruction. The culture of moral activism works to shed light on hidden or ignored injustices by uncovering them through research and analysis, hypothesizing and investigating ways of addressing them, and then passing this new knowledge of problems and solutions on to students. The culture of liberal education seeks to clarify and deepen our understanding of essential social, moral, political, intellectual, cultural, and religious questions through a fervent intellectual engagement with core traditions—studying them intensely, mining them for insight, building on them, and showing students how to do the same.

Each of the three cultures believes it properly owns the university's core ethic, and at least tacitly looks at the others as inadequate if not illegitimate. Champions of professional development often implicitly regard both liberal education and moral activism as distractions from the practical aims of higher education. Champions of liberal education speak of both professional development and moral activism as profane intrusions into what should be an almost sacred realm reserved for the pursuit of truth and beauty. Champions of moral activism treat both professional development and liberal education as callous and selfish—different forms of individual enrichment that would ignore the call of social justice.

The sum of all this—an institution largely directed at professional training, moved by an impulse for liberation from injustice, but always challenged by a small, persistent band of earnest and tradition-minded humanist gadflies—is the academic culture in America. We expect the university to take on a vast array of tasks, and we often find it embroiled in heated struggles to do so. But these struggles are easier to understand when we see that they involve internal cultures at war over the soul of the institution, and when we see that they all have legitimate, long-standing claims.

The university in America has always been suspended in different ways between the demands of such cultures. The problems that confront us on campus now are not a function of the presence of these forces but rather of the fact that the contest between them has become unbalanced, and therefore unmoored from a sense of the university's overarching institutional character and purpose. Grasping that can help us look for what is truly distinct about today's campus crisis.

THE CRISIS OF CONTEMPORARY ACADEMIC LIFE STANDS OUT AT FIRST as an atmosphere of aggressive exclusion. We are living in an era of purification on campus, undertaken in the name of an overgrown culture of moral activism. In practice, this overgrowth has often looked like the rise of an arrogant monoculture in an institution meant to foster humility and open-mindedness. Sometimes this has taken grave and ugly forms, including intellectual oppression, suppression, and exclusion—even to the point of intimidation and violence.

Incidents of verbal and physical violence have gotten the most attention, of course. These have included speakers getting shouted down or threatened on several campuses around the country, an all-out physical attack on a visiting lecturer at Middlebury College that landed a professor in the hospital, and protests at the University of Missouri in which faculty and students attacked a journalist. Sometimes the targets—such as the commentator Milo Yiannopoulos, who faced violent protests while attempting to deliver planned speeches at the University of California, Berkeley, and elsewhere— have been political provocateurs, though of course that doesn't justify threatening or attacking them. But many are just ordinary right-leaning scholars, journalists, politicians, or activists seeking to express opinions at odds with the reigning orthodoxy of campus activism. In recent years, their visits to schools across the country have begun to require security precautions that resemble the protection afforded to heads of state.

Dramatic, violent events like these have been quite rare, to be sure. But they are only the sharpest tip of an enormous iceberg. More common than such attention-grabbing incidents, and perhaps ultimately more pernicious too, is the everyday suppression of views at odds with the culture of moral activism. This can take the form of hiring decisions that appear to systematically exclude conservatives, libertarians, and even old-line liberals. It involves pressures on students to avoid expressing objections to progressive identity politics or voicing support for right-wing views. And it shows itself in a widespread sense among students, faculty, and administrators that beliefs outside the narrow bounds of the progressive campus consensus are unwelcome and can easily result in ostracism and isolation.

Conservatives have clearly long been a minority of American academics, but their numbers have dwindled to a tiny remnant in the last few decades. In 1969, a quarter of American professors described themselves as right of center, according to a study by the Carnegie Commission on Higher Education. By 1999, when the Carnegie Foundation reran the survey, the figure was down to 12 percent— even though no similar decline had occurred among the public at large. Recent surveys have put the number below one in ten, and the situation is far worse in the social sciences and the humanities. As political scientist Jon Shields noted in 2018, "By some prominent measures Republicans make up 4% of historians, 3% of sociologists, and a mere 2% of literature professors."[10]

This is a function of supply as well as demand, but the two reinforce each other. Conservatives or libertarians who are not eager to spend their careers as embattled minorities locked in endless conflict will tend to avoid disciplines where they would have so few like-minded colleagues. But a great deal of evidence and experience also suggests that those who do seek to enter these fields are often excluded. Hiring decisions in most academic programs are made by faculty committees, and, particularly in the social sciences and the humanities, there has been an undeniable pattern of exclusion. In their 2016 book *Passing on the Right: Conservative Professors in the*

Progressive University, Shields and his colleague Joshua Dunn review a great deal of evidence of both implicit and explicit marginalization of right-leaning professors in the hiring process. This kind of ideological isolation leaves right-of-center academics excluded, denies them career advancement, discourages conservative-leaning students from pursuing academic careers, and robs other students of exposure to a full range of views in some key disciplines. It is, in the end, often a kind of assertion of ownership over the university by the culture of moral activism.

It is not just self-conscious dissidents from the university's progressive culture who feel pressed in by the increasingly minute and demanding rules that govern action and speech on many campuses. The reach of that pressure into the broader campus culture is one thing that now stands out most about life in many American colleges.

From 2016 through 2018, I found myself on something of a university tour. Having authored a book about the sources of America's cultural fragmentation, I was invited to speak on the subject on a variety of campuses. Over those three years, I visited about two dozen universities, ranging from Ivy League schools and elite private colleges to small liberal-arts campuses and various state schools. I wouldn't pretend that these short visits gave me a deep understanding of college life in our time, but two distinct patterns did clearly emerge from these experiences.

One involved liberal education on campus. Again and again, in schools of different sorts in different parts of the country, when I asked my hosts (who tended to be relatively conservative faculty members or at least something like old-fashioned liberals) for their sense of campus life, they would offer some version of the view that things are awful in the American academy but that on their own particular campus they have managed to sustain a small bubble of sanity, where at least some teachers and students engage in something like traditional liberal learning. If everyone thinks their own school is an exception, they might be wrong about the rule. But that so many practitioners of liberal education feel intensely besieged and excluded is important to understand.

Talking to students, however, left me with a second and even greater worry. Simply put, students feel that they have to walk on eggshells around one another. They are exquisitely sensitive to avoid giving offense, or else, less frequently, they are driven to willfully insensitive provocations in frustration. While those driven to such provocations tend, whether as cause or effect, to tilt to the right politically, it is by no means only conservative or libertarian students who experience the pressure. Even students who generally share in the reigning progressive orthodoxy feel the burden of the code of speech and behavior, and they understand it as a code enforced by fierce peer pressure.

At the heart of this pressure is what has come to be called identity politics. On college campuses, it appears to amount to an acute emphasis on group identity and structural power relationships among different racial, ethnic, sexual, and socioeconomic camps. These relationships are understood in terms of oppressors and oppressed. As a result, the driving spirit of today's identity politics can be best understood as one of struggle against oppression. That struggle is informed by a sense that members of minority groups of all sorts are systematically mistreated—and that, as a result, their experience of life in America cannot be understood apart from that mistreatment and therefore that identity.

As the economist Arnold Kling has noted, the idea that relations of oppressor and oppressed are at the heart of social and political life is a long-standing premise of the Left in the West, while the Right tends to view politics and society through the lens of a conflict between order and disorder or civilization and barbarism. This is one reason why Left and Right sometimes talk past each other on key issues. And on American campuses, it tends to mean that identity politics is a progressive political vision that points toward progressive political agendas.[11]

But the fact that identity politics perceives people's place in and experience of American life through the lens of largely fixed group memberships means that debates about these agendas become very difficult. Challenges to the progressive conclusions of campus moralists are understood by many students as challenges to the experiences and identities of certain groups. They are understood, in other words, not as substantive political disagreements, but as modes of oppression, or at the very least as personal insults. Tying identity to politics in this particular way makes it very hard to argue about politics and to express opposing views without their being taken as attacks. To dissent is to dismiss another person's experience—indeed, to dismiss another person's very being. Such dissents are often implicitly interpreted in terms of safety and harm, and therefore treated as abuses.

This drives the best-mannered students to avoid conflict while leaving disagreement to the disagreeable alone. On college campuses, just as in our political institutions, our degraded capacity for unity and solidarity is the result of a degraded capacity for accepting differences. The trouble is not that we have forgotten how to agree but that we have forgotten how to disagree.

If we assume that, since political or cultural views are functions of personal identity, disagreement must be a function of hostility to the personal identity of another, then we must conclude that this hostility extends to that other's group, and therefore that it amounts to racism, sexism, or another form of prejudice. This understanding might be well-intentioned, but it cannot be friendly to intellectual exploration.

This became clearest to me during a visit to one particular campus in 2018. At an elite liberal-arts college in the Midwest, I was invited to attend a session of an optional one-credit course called Civil

Disagreement offered to students who lived in a specific residence hall that year. The professor and the students were very impressive—they were smart and plainly moved by goodwill. They were there by choice to think together about living respectfully with disagreement. But I couldn't help but be a little terrified by the discussion.

One after another, students reported great difficulty in navigating a terrain of intercutting cleavages of race, gender, ethnicity, and sexuality without giving offense or unknowingly stepping on landmines. They described this terrain not in a cynical way, and not as outsiders reporting on it (as I am doing here), but as significant and meaningful and yet awfully hard to manage. They seemed to exist in unending terror of saying the wrong thing to the wrong person—and not because they might be punished somehow but out of a genuine concern about giving offense or seeming insufficiently respectful of someone else's experience. They did not see this intricate social code as a barrier to civil disagreement, but as something like the setting in which they had to find ways to hear each other. There was something endearing, even impressive, about it. But this was not a world in which intellectual exploration—or much serious teaching and learning—was easy to imagine. And it didn't sound like much fun, either. It was frankly excruciating to hear. It suggested that, for these students, the university was not serving its core academic purpose: to enable a search for truth through inquiry, debate, and instruction.

This pattern of academic life—isolated islands of liberal learning in a sea of identity politics—does still make it possible for some traditional forms of liberal education (not to mention a great deal of valuable research beyond) to take place on American campuses. In terms of raw numbers, there may well be more students engaged in liberal learning today than, say, two generations ago—even if they are concentrated now in some peculiar fields like political theory and are more rarely found studying the core social sciences or humanities.

But in relation to a vastly larger academic world, liberal education seems increasingly besieged.

The tension between the culture of moral activism and the culture of liberal education reflects and magnifies the broader tensions that define the cultural conflict that pervades the larger society. The struggle between them is often not so much about how and what to learn and teach as it is about staking out platforms for performative outrage.

ON ITS FACE, EVEN THIS MAY NOT SEEM SO NEW. COLLEGE CAMPUSES, after all, were the scenes of intense protests and debates about war and peace and politics many times in our history. But echoes of past university crises, and especially those of the 1960s and 1970s, might actually obscure more than they reveal at this point. Today's institutional crisis of the university is different from those earlier ones in three especially significant ways.

First, the arrangement of forces has almost reversed itself since the 1960s. The culture of moral activism (now as then) inclines naturally toward an oppositional mind-set, and so tends to describe and understand itself as pushing against the establishment in our society and calling out the sins of the majority. But today that culture has become decidedly dominant, and not only in the university. It is far from the fringe counterculture of the '60s. Its views are shared by most of our elite institutions. In corporate America, the entertainment world, the media, throughout the professions, and across our civil society, a progressivism that leans toward identity politics is the reigning orthodoxy. And, as we have been seeing, these institutions are all increasingly functioning as arenas in the culture war. The students vocally championing identity politics today take themselves to be challenging their elders, but they are actually among the most fully assimilated elites in American life—expressing some of our society's shallowest prejudices as though they were profound, subversive insights.

Second, and much related, is another transformation in the character of the culture of moral activism in the university. Simply put: today's campus Left is more assertively moralistic than its critics tend to suggest. In warning against an increasingly militant Left on campus, conservatives have long been inclined to regard their opponents as relativists or nihilists. Identity politics and an emphasis on group differences might at first seem to fit naturally into such an understanding of the campus Left. It diminishes the search for truth, or rather treats it as relative to social status, privilege, and bias, so it does gesture toward moral relativism. A generation ago, one prominent critic of these trends described the thought process involved this way: "The human intellect cannot transcend the interests of the human body, which is white or black, male or female, heterosexual or homosexual; hence the intellect is not human in any sense that rises above those distinctions. Reason is rationalization, justification is propaganda; and therefore education is indoctrination."[12]

Such an attitude would obviously make genuine education impossible—or would render it merely a struggle for control of the implements of indoctrination. Such an understanding of today's campus battles would also mean that those battles are a direct extension of those of the 1960s.

This is surely true in some respects. But the argument masks a peculiar reversal we should notice. In the 1960s campus battles, it was the leftist activists who argued for free speech, while their conservative detractors (and targets) argued that universities required standards and boundaries, and were not just open platforms for expression of all sorts. Now the tables appear to have turned, with campus conservatives arguing for free expression and progressives insisting on setting standards and limits on what may be said and done on campus.

Maybe that's just because the progressives have gotten tenure, or because they control the commanding heights of our culture and economy. The campus activists are now in charge and eager to use their power, while the conservatives are on their heels and desperate for room to breathe. This would suggest that the fight for the soul of the university really is just a power struggle.

But by listening to the student activists, we can recognize a more consequential reversal underlying the turning of the tables on free speech. The protestors of the 1960s attacked the universities themselves as manifestations of the American establishment. They denied the university's claims to legitimacy and insisted it had no right to constrain them. They were arguing against authority, and their critics on the Right defended authority. Today's campus activists—from the Berkeley protestors insisting that right-wing speakers be banned to the Yale students demanding sanctions against racially insensitive Halloween costumes to faculty refusing to abide conservative hires—are calling on the university to exercise its legitimate authority on behalf of their moral vision for the campus. They may be wrong about what a legitimate moral vision of university life ought to be—indeed, I think they are—but they are insisting that there is one.

Radical egalitarianism is always in some danger of collapsing into relativism. But that doesn't mean the two modes of thought are the same. Some prior generations of campus activists who saw themselves as enemies of every establishment really did sometimes allow their moral passions to push them into nihilism. But the current generation of activists, perhaps because it has the elite culture at its back, is acting out of different motives and poses different risks.

In other words, today's campus activists aren't fundamentally nihilists or relativists. They are moralists. And their moral vision is hardly unfamiliar in our culture: it is a brand of radical progressive egalitarianism that speaks to some deep yearnings in the American soul. This is obviously the source of its power, and it is vital that its critics recognize that. Confounding the Left's radical egalitarianism with relativism or nihilism has been a characteristic mistake of the American Right in the last half century. It has done much to shape our politics, but it may be closest to the surface and so most significant when it comes to the culture war over the university.[13]

To describe today's campus activism in terms of coddled, over-sensitive students doesn't quite get to the heart of the matter either. As the conservative challengers and victims of campus activism know, it can be quite aggressive and confrontational. It's true that campus activists are often roused into action by speech and ideas that they find offensive, but they do not act the part of the affronted weakling.

What part do they act, then? The Puritan origins of this culture of moral activism might offer a hint. The framework of Puritan theology, echoes of which can still be found in our cultural self-understanding, offers a rich vocabulary of defilement, taboo, and purification. It is in that vocabulary that the concerns of some of today's activist culture on campus might be best understood.

As Alan Jacobs, a humanities professor at Baylor University, has put it, the activists are motivated by their commitment to an orthodoxy backed by powerful moral imperatives. They see their struggle as on behalf of the oppressed against oppressors. And they are confident that the institution of the university (along with every other institution) has a role to play in calling out the sins of the oppressors and providing protected spaces for the victims. When those spaces seem to be infiltrated by opponents—defenders of the oppressive order who are brought to campus as speakers or teachers—the activists perceive it as a defilement and therefore call for an authoritative cleansing of the protected sanctuary.[14]

Understood this way, the peculiar language employed by campus activists—a language of harm and offense, of sanctity and iniquity—

begins to make more sense. The sheer possessiveness of their approach to the campus does too. And so does the appeal of their message. Their aim, as they understand it themselves, is not to crush dissent or dominate society, let alone to relativize the core philosophical underpinnings of the West. It is to combat the systematic, structural mistreatment of oppressed groups and to recognize their distinct experiences and challenges. As they perceive it, they act on behalf of justice, and (consciously or not) they do so by deploying some of the forms of religious moralism without the content—at times almost literally the liturgy without the theology. They implicitly seek to cleanse and to redeem society through acts of performative outrage against oppression and various forms of calling out oppressors.[15]

In an age starved for liturgy (let alone for theology), this can be very powerful. The culture of activism in the university exposes students, often for the first time, to the argument that there exists a pervasive structure of social oppression in our society and simultaneously gives them means to address that injustice. It offers an entire moral system to students who feel as though society at large offers them no other such framework that they can respect. As the Aspen Institute's April Lawson has put it,

> A vacuum has opened up in campus moral culture—and in moral culture in America writ large—such that the vision offered by the social justice leaders is speaking to a deeply felt hunger. The movement's ferocity comes from this hunger, and until we find other ways to speak to it, we will find that measured, logical rejoinders à la "I agree with you that racism is a problem, I just think your way of addressing it is counterproductive" will fall on deaf ears.[16]

This doesn't mean that the moral vision offered by the activists on campus is adequate or valid—but it does mean that this vision cannot be answered by arguments for free speech alone. Freedom of speech is essential, of course. It is a prerequisite for a flourishing academic community. But it is not the purpose of that community, and so cannot be a counterargument against an unbalanced idea of what that purpose is.

What is required instead is a genuine counterbalance—a competing case about the purpose of the university, advanced in moral terms that can speak to a deep and legitimate hunger for the good and true. It must be an argument for what free inquiry and speech on campus could make possible—not simply for an undirected and unbounded freedom to say anything. It must be an argument for the university as a mold of moral character, not a platform for performative moralism.

But the third way in which today's university crisis stands out makes it especially difficult to recover that overarching academic character. The fact is that the culture of moral activism is today the dominant culture not only of a powerful faction of faculty but also of a large and growing cadre of administrators on almost every campus. This is an enormously consequential development, and may be the single most important factor in the transformation of university life.

Traditionally, university administration has implicitly been dominated by the culture of professional development, and its practitioners have tried to keep the peace on campus by focusing students on practical goals, satisfying parents and trustees, and raising money. This has often been frustrating to champions of both liberal education and social activism on campus, who have reveled in describing administrators as shallow and unimaginative. But in recent decades, this practical approach to university administration has given way to a style that keeps the peace by making progressive social activism the official code of university life.

There is great functional power in this approach, because it allows administrators to wield immense social pressure as a management tool—calling out troublemakers and subjecting them to enormous risks of ostracism, keeping dissenters in line, and weakening competing power centers on campus. But this power is generally not explicitly exercised with such Machiavellian motives. It is the genuinely held worldview of the rising generation of college administrators, and it has come to shape the expectations of students as well.

These students now perceive the ideological suppositions of campus social activism as a plausible administrative framework for a large institution, and when they graduate, they often carry those expectations with them into the other elite institutions they come to inhabit—in the professional world (as we saw in the last chapter), the civic sector, government, and elsewhere. This is one way in which the transformation of campus culture has helped fuel the larger transformations we are tracing. It helps account for the peculiar demands that younger workers in these elite institutions—from Silicon Valley to Wall Street, from Hollywood to Washington— now routinely make of their often bewildered new employers. Talk to anyone in management in an elite, white-collar company and you'll hear stories of the youngest employees expecting the company to enforce a code of political correctness utterly unfamiliar in the world of work until the last few years. The reason for that is not so much that activist professors taught them to think this way as that activist administrators taught them to understand authority this way.

Talking to right-leaning faculty on campus after campus, I have been struck by their perception of this trend. They often do not blame their colleagues first and foremost for the exclusion and hostility they face. They entered the academy expecting to encounter Marxist literature professors and assorted technocratic liberals at faculty meetings. The problem, as they frequently see it, is that administrators have become enforcers of a social-activist orthodoxy, and in a way that undermines the basic character of the university as an institution.

The university should be administered by a party of the academy, not by one of the parties to the culture war.

TODAY'S CAMPUS TENSIONS ARE ULTIMATELY ROOTED IN THE DISTOR-tion of the fundamental institutional character of the academy by an increasingly hyperaggressive culture of activism. That culture is certainly formative—it shapes the students who come under its influence. But it is not itself sufficiently formed by the overarching purpose of the institution, and so it shapes those students in ways that answer to the broader culture war and not to the purpose of the university.

That purpose is ultimately the discovery, development, amass-ing, examination, and application of knowledge—pursued through teaching and learning. The question that can help us judge the appro-priateness or integrity of what happens on campus is something like "Are we building knowledge?" It is not just whether something you propose to do will get you a job, or will make our society more just, or is fulfilling and enjoyable, but whether what you propose to do involves teaching and learning in pursuit of some knowledge of the truth. If it does not, it probably does not belong in the university. And if it does, then, even if it makes us uncomfortable, it is a function of the university. That doesn't offer a simple formula for thinking about everything that happens on campus, but it offers a useful rule of thumb for making judgments.

This rule of thumb does not point toward free speech as such but toward academic freedom that enables academic life. It can help us tell the difference, for instance, between giving time and attention on campus to a pure political provocateur and troll who just wants to get a rise out of people and giving time to an accomplished social sci-entist who offers arguments backed with evidence that people may not like to hear. It can also mark the difference between social activism pursued by honest inquiry and social activism that shuts down dissent and represses discussion.

Even when it is focused on social change, activism can be an application of academic insights. Campus struggles for greater racial equality or in opposition to war have often involved applying the lessons of academic life to a larger social purpose. In the late 1960s, for example, the great sociologist Seymour Martin Lipset noted a common distinction in this regard between white and black college activists. "Black student protest," he wrote, "differs considerably from that of the more affluent white radicals in that the politics of the former is much more instrumental, directed toward realistic, achievable goals, whereas that of the latter is inclined to be expressive, more oriented toward showing up the 'immorality' of the larger society than to securing attainable reforms."[17]

Today's culture of moral activism on campus is almost entirely "expressive" in this sense, and as such it is not only not sufficiently political but also not sufficiently academic. Teaching and learning are not frequently enough its means, which puts it at odds with the character of the larger institution and therefore with the other cultures that populate that institution.

The American academy has always existed in a balance between these cultures, and that balance is now under threat by a performative notion of the purpose of the university. To recover a constructive tension between them, we would have to recover an idea of the university as more of a mold than a platform. In this sense, we ought to see that the university crisis of our time is at least partly a function of a larger transformation of attitudes about the roles of institutions in our society—a transformation that has led many academics to think of their own institutions as stages for moralistic performance of the same sort that increasingly dominates politics, the media, the professions, and much else.

Critics of the campus moralists, meanwhile, have tended to respond to their excesses with a counterculture of performance, and a demand for platforms for themselves. They too should see that more is required of them in the current crisis. Combating the rise of a kind of moral activism destructive to the purpose of the university would mean fighting for the properly formed and formative character of the institution. For those committed to a culture of liberal education on campus, this means not just demanding safe spaces or giving the impression that instead of one view on every question there ought to be two. Liberal education has much more to offer than that. Showing what it has to offer—showing in an attractive, engaged, appealing way how to fill the spaces opened up by academic freedom, not just how to keep them open—is the challenge that now confronts defenders of the university.

They may find some allies in this struggle among champions of the culture of professional development, who after all have no interest in seeing campuses devolve into political war zones. They may even find allies among the moral activists, some of whom are clearly committed to a genuinely academic ideal of the university. But above all they should seek and are likely to find allies among students, parents, trustees, donors, and interested citizens who grasp the value of the university as an institution with different modes and cultures, but with an overarching aim essential to the future of our society.

They should seek to direct the energy of these allies not only toward sustaining some pockets of liberal learning in the substantive work of the academy but also, and crucially, toward forging a party of the university among administrators. The culture of liberal learning and the culture of professional development need to engage in a self-conscious project to recapture and reform university administration, by pursuing administrative posts, engaging with administrators in ways that give them incentives to come along, and appealing to the constituencies that administrators can't ignore. They must appeal to a notion of the university as an institution of learning and teaching, not just ask for equal time in an endless political and cultural conflict where the university is one more arena. The struggle over the university must be a struggle *for* the university—not just for control of it but for the preservation of its character and purpose in an age that relentlessly strives to distract us from both.

six

THE INFORMALITY MACHINE

WHEN FUTURE GENERATIONS LOOK BACK UPON THE EARLY decades of the twenty-first century, they will surely wonder at the bizarre spectacle of our society driving itself mad on social media. From high-school students subjecting one another to horrific bullying online, to our political and media elites abandoning all patience and decorum in an endless barrage of tantrums and counter-tantrums, to paranoid conspiracy theorists gaining traction and legitimacy, to foreign governments picking at the rifts and scabs of our society, social media has exposed and exacerbated some grievous vulnerabilities.

These same social media platforms have also played a prominent role in the transformation of institutions that we have been tracing. Again and again, as formative institutions are deformed into performative ones, the role of social media is hard to ignore.

It is worth asking why that should be, because the role of social media in the transformation of our institutions can offer insights about what those institutions really are and do. On the face of things, we might expect social media to strengthen our institutions, because the avowed purpose of social media platforms is to supplement our social lives: to connect people, to help us communicate and organize, and thus to help us do things more easily together. Social media has done all of that for many of us, without question. But as political scientist Joshua Mitchell has noted, in practice social media platforms have often also become a substitute for our social lives, and as such have done nearly the opposite of what we might hope: pulling us apart, encouraging aggression and hostility, and keeping us from hearing each other.[1]

What does this tell us about how to understand social media as media—that is, as what stands between people and connects them? What does the particular sort of mediation that social media offers do to our relationships, to the way we understand ourselves, and to our ways of thinking about others? And why is it that our social media platforms seem to be such a great fit for the vices and dysfunctions of our time but such a poor fit for efforts to recover institutional integrity, civic peace, and solidarity?

TO CONSIDER THESE QUESTIONS, WE SHOULD BEGIN WITH A LITTLE more clarity about just what we mean when we say "social media." The term is capacious, and the phenomenon takes many forms.

In a broad, functional sense, the term refers to internet-based applications that facilitate the exchange of information in ways that create chosen virtual communities. The various platforms of social media (today, Facebook, Instagram, YouTube, and Twitter might be considered the characteristic examples, but this has changed with time and will change again) usually require users to create profiles by which they will be known and identified. The platform then enables them to connect with other users and to exchange text, images, video, and the like. Users often build circles of people with whom the platform keeps them in touch, and so are part of social networks of various shapes and sizes.

Within these networks, exchanges often take the simple form of expression and feedback: a user puts something before his or her followers, and they respond—generally with some form of vague applause or affirmation, sometimes with disapproval or contention. Either way, the basic model involves the creation of a self-contained social space in which we can display or express ourselves before others and receive immediate reactions.

The appeal of such instantaneous response is enormous, particularly when our circle of followers or friends is likely to affirm rather than criticize us. The effect can easily become downright addictive—every like and retweet feels like sweet acceptance. Responding to the displays of others is often a type of performance too, whether that means publicly showing solidarity with a view we want to be seen affirming or projecting outrage at those with whom we disagree. Delivering such a reaction can be just as intensely satisfying as receiving it. The whole experience can be to real social life what a drug-induced high is to real joy: a quick, intense substitute that feels for a moment like the real thing while actually keeping us from it.

Of course, that isn't all we do on social media. A lot of our time on these platforms is spent communicating in more traditional ways—exchanging information, keeping up with family and friends, learning something, being entertained. But what has been truly distinct about social media, and truly disruptive, has more to do with the tendency to substitute display and response for communication.

That substitution points us to the peculiar idea of sociality that has shaped these platforms and been shaped by them. Mark Zuckerberg, the founder of Facebook, has been unusually articulate about this idea. He is careful always to describe Facebook users as a "community" and believes, as he put it in a 2017 manifesto for the company, that "Facebook stands for bringing us closer together and building a global community." The role of the platform, in Zuckerberg's vision, is fundamentally infrastructural. As he wrote,

> In times like these, the most important thing we at Facebook can do is develop the social infrastructure to give people the power to build a global community that works for all of us. For the past decade, Facebook has focused on connecting friends and families. With that foundation, our next focus will be developing the social infrastructure for community—for supporting us, for keeping us safe, for informing us, for civic engagement, and for inclusion of all.

Zuckerberg evinces a serious awareness of the fact that "social media can contribute to divisiveness and isolation," and he expresses a desire to enable Facebook to support rather than displace traditional communal structures. Noting the decline in participation in civic institutions over recent decades, he writes that "online communities are a bright spot, and we can strengthen existing physical communities by helping people come together online as well as offline." Articulating an idea of social media as supportive and supplemental of community, he concludes, "In a world where this physical social infrastructure has been declining, we have a real opportunity to help strengthen these communities and the social fabric of our society."[2]

Zuckerberg's desire to use Facebook to reinforce what he calls "physical social infrastructure" with something like virtual social infrastructure suggests a sense that some of the problems we confront are functions of a decline of our core social institutions. But this desire, like similar assertions by other leading voices in social media, seems rooted in an understanding of the problem that overlooks its basic character. The notion that "helping people come together online as well as offline" will be an effective means of addressing the crisis suggests that the crisis involves, at a fundamental level, an inability to come together. If that were so, then a technology that allows us to connect would surely help a lot. But *how* we come together matters. The titans of social media seem to have given remarkably little attention to the ways in which their platforms actually structure interaction—or at least to how these ways of structuring social life add up to something like a social psychology.

What they have thought about—quite a bit, in fact—is how they might structure the incentives users face on their platforms to maximize attention, which after all is the commodity they offer. Facebook's "global community" of users consists not of paying customers but of people who have access to the platform at no cost. Its paying customers are advertisers, to whom the company sells the attention (and sometimes personal information) of those users. There is nothing inherently wrong with such a business model—advertising-based media companies have been with us for centuries. But those companies have generally understood themselves not as facilitators of social interaction but as providers of information or entertainment. That's much of what the social media platforms are too, but it's not how they ultimately understand themselves or how users understand them. Mediating our social lives through information and entertainment platforms suggests we understand our social lives as forms of mutual entertainment and information. And the more of our social lives that we launder through such platforms, the more this peculiar understanding of sociality becomes the truth.

The demands of the business model of most social media companies further distort our understanding of the social. They need us to pay brief but repeated attention to the platform, so that we are in a position to be exposed to what advertisers want to tell us. In order to draw us in and to keep us coming back, Facebook and other social media companies work to appeal to our impulses and desires in ways designed to form a kind of staccato serial dependence. This often involves encouraging short bursts of intense interaction, promoting behaviors (like virtue signaling, shaming, or aggressive confrontation) that can be indulged in brief spurts and yet are deeply appealing, and boosting the sort of shallow affirmation of our biases that has a shot at going viral and so of drawing in lots more attention from large groups of people. This is what keeps us coming back. While this makes a lot of sense as a way of creating a ready viewer base for advertising, it makes little sense as a way of creating an environment for social interaction.

The two imperatives that confront the designers of social media experiences—to build the infrastructure for community and to build a reliable base of potential customers for advertisers—are thus obviously in tension. That tension is magnified by the sheer, astonishing scale of social media. Here, too, Facebook is the most useful illustration, since—although its users tend to be older than the average social media devotee—it is currently the largest of the social media platforms. As *New York* magazine's Max Read has put it, "At 2 billion members, 'monthly active Facebook users' is the single largest non-biologically sorted group of people on the planet after 'Christians.'" Just under a third of the people on earth are Facebook users—even though the platform is essentially banned in China, the world's most populous country. The breadth and scope of what happens on the platform, from sharing photos with friends and relatives to organizing protests in despotic regimes to the dissemination of news to tens of billions of dollars in advertising to state-sponsored election interference—and lots in between—practically defies comprehension.[3]

Twitter's "community" of users is far smaller than Facebook's but still quite substantial, at more than three hundred million active monthly users (though that is the number of accounts, and, unlike Facebook, Twitter permits multiple accounts per user). Whatever its exact user base, though, Twitter is especially popular with professionals and opinion shapers in America and thus plays a huge role in how our political, cultural, intellectual, media, and entertainment elites spend their time. Both platforms, along with others like Instagram (owned by Facebook) and YouTube (owned by Google), have grown in scale with stunning speed and come to play a dominant role in the formation of culture and the shaping of politics and media.

In the blink of an eye, these large social media platforms have created an entirely new arena of human interaction unlike any we have known. The culture of that arena, which we barely understand, cannot help but influence our larger culture in some perverse and unexpected ways, and will only become more influential with time. We are just now beginning to get a sense of its effects on our society's core institutions.

THE SIMPLEST IRONY OF THE ERA OF SOCIAL MEDIA IS THAT THE platforms intended to help people come together have often pulled us apart. If any single term can describe the ethos of our time, the very age in which social media has flowered, it would be isolation. In some important respects, this has been an age of isolation not despite but because of social media.

Part of the reason for this is that the idea of connection at the heart of social media tends to be thin and ephemeral. It offers a form of connection that consists of quick, momentary communication rather than relationships of mutual dependence. Indeed, this is true of how the internet more generally has tended to reshape various kinds of human connection. E-commerce tends to offer us convenience and efficiency by eliminating the need for various kinds of human interaction and connection. It enables us to shop without seeing or speaking to anyone, and so to be left alone while getting what we want or need. Some of the most distinct innovators in the tech sector (like Uber, Airbnb, WeWork, and others) create opportunities for temporary, on-demand choices that enable us to avoid enduring commitments to standing institutions. We just use what we need when we need it and move on, and our interactions with service providers are very limited.

Snapchat offers the epitome of this approach in the realm of social media—allowing users to send messages that quickly disappear once they are viewed. But Twitter has much the same effect. Even Facebook offers relationships of pure communication among disembodied profiles rather than of connection with other individuals. In such a realm, we can hear and be heard but we rarely really talk to people.

One problem with this way of interacting is that it leaves many of us with the sense that our social lives do not allow us to engage very deeply with anyone. We all want desperately to be known by the people in our lives—to be understood, sympathized with, related to, and appreciated. But the more that we subcontract our relationships to these forms of mediation that flatten our interactions, the fewer opportunities we have to be truly known, even by friends, and to know other people. The sense of being connected but lonely, in touch but untouched, is pervasive in the age of social media, and it is hard to overcome on the platforms.[4]

Not only *who* but *what* we know can be dangerously constrained by social media. Among the most valuable benefits of living in society is the miracle of serendipitous learning: finding ourselves exposed to knowledge or opinion or wisdom or beauty that we did not seek out and would never have known to expect. This kind of experience is not only a way to broaden our horizons and learn about the ways and views of others, it is also an utterly essential component of what we might call socialization. Being constantly exposed to influences we did not choose is part of how we learn to live with others, to accept our differences while seeing crucial commonalities, to realize the world is not all about us, and to at least abide with patience what we would rather avoid or escape.

We should not underestimate the socializing power of such un-chosen experience. As the great mid-century urbanist Jane Jacobs suggested, this is a way in which the city creates the urbane denizen it requires. It is similarly the way in which our society more generally creates the kind of sophisticated liberal citizen that can be trusted with the immense degree of freedom our way of life provides us. We should therefore not underestimate the consequences of being able to cordon ourselves off into hermetically sealed bubbles filled with only the exposures and experiences we select—or those that various clever algorithms serve up for us.[5]

Such algorithms are a particularly important source of this loss of serendipity online. They are designed to predict our preferences, and so to ensconce us in exposures and experiences we might have cho-sen, rather than ones we would never have known to want. They af-firm us rather than shape us. Therefore, they are forms of expression more than means of formation. We might say that in moving large portions of our social lives from the streets of the city to the arena of social media, we move ourselves almost literally from a mold onto a platform.

Even our consumption of information and knowledge now has come to be an expressive act. Facebook explains its news feed to its users this way: "If you could look through thousands of stories ev-ery day and choose the 10 that were most important to you, which would they be? The answer should be your News Feed. It is subjec-tive, personal, and unique—and defines the spirit of what we hope to achieve."[6]

Of course, the user doesn't really choose the stories that com-pose his or her feed; Facebook does the choosing, but it does it in a way designed to predict what the user would have wanted. The goal, in other words, is to reinforce what you already know, enjoy, and believe, and so to make you more like you already are. Some other platforms don't engineer your experience quite so aggressively, but they still let you choose your circle of people to follow and allow you to avoid exposure to unwanted voices. That's obviously part of the appeal of social media. But it is also part of the problem with it.

This shortage of serendipity not only means we are less frequently exposed to new ideas or challenges to our expectations. It also means we are constantly exposed to our own chosen circle in a way that intensifies the power and emotional valence of peer pressure. Social media often involves strong, unmitigated peer pressure, which can range from a quiet voice constantly repeating the conventional wisdom of our circle to a harsh, unforgiving enforcement of orthodoxy that demands we affirm and reaffirm the views and judgments of our kind and display the approved reactions to various totems and slogans. The platforms let us display ourselves, but what we display had better be proof that we are part of our crowd, or else the consequences could be serious.

A similar pattern shows itself in how we consume information online. The lively exchange of news and opinion on social media platforms has made them a foremost source of information about the world for many people. But because these platforms are designed to let us select and control whom and what we are exposed to, the exchange of information tends to devolve quickly into a process of iterative confirmation bias, by which people exchange and reexchange information with like-minded friends in a way that tends to intensify the impression that the information is reliable without the benefit of external validation. This is precisely why social media platforms are so attractive to advertisers, but it is also why they are very poorly suited to serve as news providers. This process affirms our preconceptions while giving us the impression that we are becoming informed, and can easily leave everyone involved knowing less and less about the real world.

In this respect, social media can of course be quite formative, but in ways that reinforce our current form rather than refining it. This is particularly problematic as these platforms come to replace more of our experience of the broader world—to stand in for the formative experiences and connections of the public sphere. What happens on social media, in this sense, isn't quite public. It occurs in a space you design to your liking.

Yet, that space is not quite private either, and it denies us some key benefits of private social interactions. As social media consists of a set of platforms, it is not well suited to intimacy of any sort. This may seem a strange observation. After all, in some respects the online world seems overflowing with intimacy: everyone shares very personal information—from pictures of their children to provocative opinions and jokes and complaints to extremely private dating profiles and intimate photos and messages. Exchanges of views on social media also have a way of falling into displays and responses that seem very direct and personal. As Stephen Marche has put it, "Every Twitter or Facebook discussion inevitably descends from an external subject—organic farming, video games, poetry—to interpersonal griping: 'your tone is insulting' or 'who do you think you are?' Politics on the internet indulges a hatred for the other side that's unprecedented in its intimacy and ferocity. 'Those people are scum' and 'I hate your guts' are the principal political messages of the era of digital connectivity."[7]

But "personal" is actually very different from intimate, or even private. In fact, the realm of social media often effectively functions as an arena for saying private things in public, and thereby confounding the public and the private in a way that renders social interactions deeply uneasy and unsatisfying. Some people, especially those who have grown up in the digital era, are sufficiently accustomed to this confusion that they do not even recognize it. They behave online as they might among their closest friends, even if a much broader circle of people can see them. This can have serious consequences—ranging from personal embarrassment to professional ruin or worse. But even people who seem perfectly at home with this peculiar ambiguity are often left starved for social intimacy and denied the opportunity to really let their guard down.

This confusion of public and private (rather than the kinds of worries we often hear about surveillance or the exposure of personal information) is the real privacy crisis of the internet age. It is a defining feature of social media, and of life in our era more generally. It is just not easy to say whether what happens online is exactly private or public, and the reason for that uncertainty is a kind of informality driven by the structure of social media itself.

ALTHOUGH WE OFTEN CANNOT TELL IF THE WORLD OF SOCIAL MEDIA is public or private, indeed precisely because we cannot tell, we can certainly call what happens in that world *informal*. We might even think of social media as a massive informality machine, robbing our interactions of structure and of boundaries. This is why moving more of our social activities onto the platforms of social media tends to bring the most dramatic and fundamental changes to those of our social interactions that would otherwise be most formal—like the presentation of professional work product, the intricate dance of dating and courtship, or the pronouncements of public policy. It is also why social media is uniquely corrosive of institutions, which are after all precisely social forms.

Formality has a bad name in our relentlessly democratic culture—we tend to equate it with stuffiness and rigidity. Informality, on the other hand, is synonymous with authenticity. But another way of understanding formality might be as a means of fitting social form to social function. It is a way of behaving when something important is at stake, which sends a signal regarding that importance, establishes a framework for its integrity and structure, and lends credence and protection to all involved.

From the formal vote that indicates a decision at a meeting to the letterhead that signifies the authority of an official notice to the structure of a scientific claim, formalities distinguish the exercise of legitimate power. They send us vital signals about what to take seriously and what to take lightly, when to speak and when to listen, who to trust and who to question. They offer us an architecture of behavior that makes it possible to have some predictability and security in high-stakes situations so we might successfully navigate the social world.

Online, all of these forms are abandoned. Everyone is just an individual on a platform. The results can be great fun, but also very dangerous and confusing. The informality makes it hard for us to tell different kinds of expression apart, to judge what to believe, and to know how to behave. People often cross boundaries they would never think of crossing in an even slightly formal interaction in the offline world. Online, we frequently feel the painful absence of those barriers and boundaries.

The formalities of our social relations often mediate between individuals for their protection. They ensure, for example, that anonymity cannot be combined with proximity. If you communicate with someone directly, they know who is speaking to them; if you communicate anonymously, there will be some distance between the two of you. But on social media and in the online world, the absence of formal structures of mediation often translates to anonymity combined with proximity—and that combination can be perilous and toxic.

Anyone with even a modest public profile today can relate harrowing stories of nasty and pernicious harassment by anonymous trolls. Whether on Twitter (which allows for essentially anonymous profiles), in online comments on published writing, or by email, the internet often serves as a kind of open sewer pipe, spewing streams of excrement upon anyone who expresses an opinion in public.

Anonymity relieves internet trolls of any need for the restraint that might be called for in the real world—out of concern for one's reputation, for example, or just from the healthy discomfort involved in treating someone else horribly. This is surely why people behave online in ways they would never contemplate in their offline lives.

In the course of the 2016 election, for instance, I found myself on the receiving end of intense and ugly anti-Semitism from various critics of my political writing, and discovered that essentially every Jewish writer I knew could say the same. Others face far worse. Women with public profiles seem to suffer the most heinous abuses, often including abject threats of horrendous sexual violence—almost always anonymously.

But anonymity is not the only way that informality creates real problems on social media. In many cases, people who are not anonymous at all behave in online exchanges in ways they never would in face-to-face conversations. The reason is not so much the absence of a tangible human connection as the absence of mediation. That absence is why we so often find professionals acting unprofessionally online, and why people in positions of authority or prominence so frequently forget their responsibilities and allow themselves to get dragged into the mud.

Many of the elites who shape our culture, economy, and politics have allowed themselves in recent years to be plucked out of the various institutions that normally refine and structure their work and to be plopped instead as individuals, unconstrained and unprotected, onto the exposed platforms of social media. Indeed, they have rushed to do this to themselves. We have noticed this pattern already in each of the institutions considered in earlier chapters. The performative excesses that we traced there—which have distorted the roles played by political leaders, journalists, scientists, and other professionals—are most often found on social media. Social media has replaced academic exchanges of ideas with culture-war salvos on university campuses. It has confounded relationships formed within communities and among neighbors. It has made it hard to know what to believe. And it has helped to turn countless different sorts of institutions into interchangeable stages for the same kind of cultural psychodrama—flattening the distinct forms and formalities of each.[8]

The result is a loss of both restraint and protection—both of which are made possible by robust institutions. As individuals exposed on the platforms, we are always at risk of being betrayed by our own impulses and becoming ridiculous. The discipline and reticence so essential to leadership, professionalism, responsibility, decency, and maturity are forcefully discouraged by the incentives of the online world. Yet we all seem to find those incentives impossible to resist.

All of this results in a blurring of boundaries. Not only are the boundaries between public and private effectively erased in the realm of social media, but so are the boundaries between inside and out—that is, between the relative security of the inner lives of our institutions and the wilderness of our popular culture.

The breakdown of these barriers is everywhere apparent. Where politics ends and entertainment begins is increasingly difficult to say; the lines between activism, journalism, and conspiracy mongering are increasingly blurry; the boundary between academic research and political argument is too. In this way, our culture seems increasingly at war with itself everywhere, because the lines between the appropriate and the inappropriate arenas for such combat grow confounded. The internal cultures of many corporations are now hard to tell apart from those of college campuses, which in turn seem an awful lot like those of political movements.

The result might be described as a confusion of two notions of roles. People have roles to play inside institutions. But playing a role is also what an actor does, to tell a story to an audience. The first kind of role describes an obligation shaped by constraints; the second is a mode of expression put on for show. These two kinds of role-play have become thoroughly muddled in our public life, and the ethos of reality television (in which it is never quite clear if we are watching people live their real lives or act for our amusement) has come to dominate our experience.

Is this real or is it for show? That question has long hung like a cloud over celebrity culture. We have always had a vague sense that what we see of the lives of movie stars and other cultural icons is somehow choreographed. The same is true now of our politicians—who seem increasingly willing to be seen reading a script or playing a role with a half wink to the crowd. As we noted in chapter 3, politics practiced this way is utterly corrosive of the ethos of republican government. If people involved in the political world play roles in the sense that actors do, it becomes nearly impossible for them to play roles in the sense that leaders and citizens do. And the same can be said of many other institutions. The ambiguity of celebrity theatrics now confounds vast swaths of our culture.

In fact, the specter of celebrity culture, which we have encountered again and again as a foil to institutional culture, is a very useful lens through which to think about what happens on social media. By letting us carefully curate the image of ourselves available to others, social media encourages us to think of ourselves as living performatively. As we are experiencing an important milestone in our lives, or just enjoying a beautiful day with family or friends, a great many of us find ourselves thinking about how to capture this moment for Instagram or Facebook. As we undergo some mass experience of tragedy or joy or surprise, we work to convey an appealing image of ourselves experiencing it. Any time we are confronted with frustration—a delayed flight, an idiot boss, bad service some-where—we yearn for a platform to vent our irritation to the world. When we find ourselves in some particularly lovely or notable place, or in the company of someone our circle of friends might know, we reach for the phone not to capture that person or place but to cap-ture ourselves in proximity to them. The selfie culture is a culture of personalized micro-celebrity, in which we each act as our own paparazzi, relentlessly trading in our own privacy for attention and affirmation and turning every moment into a show.

Half a century ago, the historian Daniel J. Boorstin famously defined a celebrity as "a person known for being well-known." The celebrity in this sense, Boorstin argued, was a result of our cultural evolution from a folk society to a mass society—so that our heroes went from being people more virtuous and able than the rest of us, known for great deeds, to being people just like the great mass of us but known for great fame. Today, as our culture continues to evolve from a mass society toward a more customized, personal-ized, self-focused ideal, we want to move from just all gawking at celebrities in common to each of us being a celebrity on our own. Our technology lets us do that, creating the custom form of the distinct mass hero. The platforms of social media offer each of us the means and the incentives to act as a celebrity before our own circle of followers. As a result, we sometimes find it hard to really feel like we are living our lives unless we know others are watching us live them.[9]

This is deeply strange. But it is an extension of the very trends we have been tracing through a range of institutions. The breaking down of the barriers between inside and out, private and public, for-mal and informal, tends inexorably to leave us isolated, exposed—lacking the benefits of both intimacy and the public square—and voracious for sources of belonging and meaning and for some sense of relation and place.

Just as our social lives and cultural interactions have become confused in this process, so our institutions have been weakened. The process that pulls us out of distinct institutional roles and puts us on display as individuals has increasingly robbed our institutions of their inner lives. When a controversy arises within a company or school or charity or agency, the kinds of discussions that might once have happened in private among people mutually committed to the aims of the institution now often take place on social media, where there is little room for accommodation and patience. In this respect, too, the line between public and private is blurred, so that people often say openly what might have been better aired behind closed doors. This makes it hard for parties of the institution to form internally, since it pressures people to take sides publicly and treat the institution as an arena for partisan disagreement. This is now a key part of the process by which our institutions come to be transformed from molds to platforms.

ALL OF THIS SEEMS AWFULLY GRIM AND DISCONCERTING. A WHOLE host of novel problems are now sprouting around a set of technologies that were well intentioned and that offer some real benefits too. These problems exacerbate some of the most troubling trends in our national life and in so doing create deep, festering dysfunctions that we sometimes seem powerless to escape.

It may be, of course, that our society will develop novel antibodies to this set of problems in the coming years. After all, the internet and social media have not been around that long—and we are only now learning to live with them. Just as the first generations of human beings who lived packed together in cities faced all manner of new social difficulties, so we early denizens of the online world find ourselves confronted with bizarre and unexpected maladies. But over time, as we recognize these problems, we may find ways to live with them, and to enjoy the benefits of information technologies while minimizing some of these costs.[10]

I have found some reasons for hope in this regard in my own recent experience. I run a policy journal that often hires young editors out of college. A decade ago, perusing the social media profiles of potential hires often turned up a slew of outrageously embarrassing revelations—all manner of statements, photos, and exchanges that no one should want potential employers or the world at large to see but that were left in the open and publicly accessible. This happens far more rarely now. It seems that over just a few years, younger people have learned some of the risks of overexposure and careless social media habits. Our potential hires today are probably just taking better care to keep their profiles more private, or to use different profiles for different audiences. They may be no less corrupted by social media, even if they are more private about it. But that in itself is a sign that we are learning to live in this new environment and might gradually evolve to protect ourselves against its worst excesses. The simple fact that our social media platforms have brought with them some serious problems is no longer really news to anyone. This is another reason to think we will approach them more soberly and mitigate some of the trouble they bring.

And yet, there is no denying that the social media platforms have undercut our social lives. They plainly encourage the vices most dangerous to a free society. They drive us to speak without listening, to approach others confrontationally rather than graciously, to spread conspiracies and rumors, to dismiss and ignore what we would rather not hear, to make the private public, to oversimplify a complex world, to react to one another much too quickly and curtly. They eat away at our capacity for patient toleration, our decorum, our forbearance, our restraint. They leave us open to manipulation—by merchants, algorithms, even real-life Russian agents. They cause us to mistake expression for reflection, affirmation for respect, and reaction for responsibility. They grind down our democratic soul.

We all see this in ourselves, and we need to pull back from it. That would mean consciously reducing the time we spend on these platforms and curtailing our dependence on their cheap affirmation. But it must mean more than that too. Our social media platforms function as anti-institutions, and to address the problems they create we need to reinvest ourselves in the lives of our institutions. We should not ignore, and need not abandon, the benefits that social media and the internet provide. But we must view them as supplements, not substitutes, to the work our institutions do. And that would mean recommitting to that work.

seven

CLOSE TO HOME

THE SOCIAL CRISIS THAT HAS SENT US ON THIS EXPEDITION through our institutions is first and foremost a crisis of the interpersonal. It shows itself in isolation, alienation, failures of responsibility, and scarcities of belonging and solidarity. In considering its causes, we have surveyed political, professional, academic, and cultural institutions—and in each case, we found that Americans increasingly expect institutions not to form and socialize the people within them but rather to display those people and provide them with arenas for self-expression.

This pattern leads to dangerous deformations across our society. But we might expect that it would be particularly harmful to institutions whose character is most intensely interpersonal—the institutions of family, religion, and community. Such institutions, even more than those of government, the media, or the academy, become less like themselves when they mutate into venues for preening or homogenized arenas for political-cultural combat. And yet, these most personal and interpersonal of our institutions are also those that must above all be recovered if we are to address the social challenges we confront. Because they form us on a more fundamental level than any of our other institutions, they are needed to help each of us form the kind of character required of free citizens. It is these institutions that are most crucial and effective in fighting isolation, alienation, and loneliness by enabling people to build the most personal connections, loyalties, and affinities. We now suffer from a shortage of what they provide even as we undermine their ability to provide it. So we would do well to conclude our tour of some illustrative institutions with a few of those nearest to home—where the trouble is greatest, but where answers must start.[1]

THE IDEA THAT THE FAMILY IS AN INSTITUTION AT ALL IS HARD TO deny and yet difficult to comprehend. This is in part because the family occupies a distinct space between two meanings of the term "institution." It is not an organization exactly, but neither is it quite a practice or a set of rules or norms. In a sense, the family is a collection of several institutions understood in this latter way—like the institution of marriage and the institution of parenthood. The family arranges these institutions into a coherent and durable structure that is almost a formal organization. It resists easy categorization because it is primeval. The family has a legal existence, but it is decidedly pre-legal. It has a political significance, but it is pre-political too. It is pre-everything.

This is sometimes a real problem for our liberal society, because it casts doubt upon the idea that our natural state is some kind of libertarian individualism. Some important political theorists in our liberal tradition have tried to ground their ideal of liberty in a pre-social condition, or a state of nature, that is populated by wholly independent individuals. Yet these kinds of thought experiments, for all their value, are plainly implausible as descriptions of the human condition. No human being has ever lived a life in circumstances of utter individualism, without some degree of community—which often is at first an extended family. Our social order flows out of the basic conditions of how we come into the world, move through it, and depart it, and so it unavoidably flows outward from the family. Family is the most primordial, and therefore the most foundational, of the institutions that form a society.

It is also therefore, more than anything else in our experience, a *form* of our common life—a structure for doing essential things together. That is what makes it our most basic institution. But how is the form of the family related to its function? It is this seemingly straightforward question that has put the family at the center of our contemporary culture wars.

We know that people need thriving families to flourish. No one in any corner of our politics would really deny that now. But what are the needs that the family meets? Some are surely practical necessities: families care for their members' material needs. They feed and house children (and at times the elderly or others) who would be unable to feed and house themselves. They enable the sharing of resources and responsibilities, so that everyone has someone whom they trust, and whom the larger society trusts, to care for them if they are unable to care for themselves. The family is also a vessel for our deepest loves: it is a formal acknowledgment of a set of human relationships.

These two facets of what the family does—serving as a means of provision and a means of recognition—are increasingly central to our contemporary understanding of the family's function. But they leave out the family's formative purpose, the ways in which it shapes our soul and molds our character. When we put aside the formative functions of the family, we might be able to persuade ourselves that thriving families are important only for economic and symbolic reasons—that so long as our material needs are met and our relationships are recognized, the family has served its core purposes. Where families prove unable to meet their members' material needs, other forms of assistance, both public and private, can fill in the gap, and the family can just stand as an acknowledgment of mutual love among its members.

This would suggest that the form of the family, and therefore its formative potential, may not be essential to its function. But, of all our institutions, this is surely nowhere less true than in the family. The family is our first and most important institution, not only from the perspective of the history of humanity, but also (and more simply) in the life of every individual. It is where we enter the world, literally where we alight when we depart the womb. It gives us our first impression of the world, and our first understanding of what it is all about. It then sees us through some of our most vulnerable years of life, taking us by the hand as we progress from the formless ignorance of the newborn through the formative innocence of early childhood to the fearful insecurities of juvenile transformations and hopefully, eventually, to a formed and mature adjusted posture in society. This is a process of socialization, and therefore fundamentally of formation. But it is not a formation that happens through instruction so much as through example and habituation. The family forms us by imprinting its forms upon us and giving us models to emulate and patterns to adopt.

The family does all this by giving each of its members a role, a set of relations to others, a body of responsibilities, and a network of privileges. Each of these, in its own way, is given more than earned and is obligatory more than chosen. Although the core human relationship at the heart of most families—the marital relationship—is one we enter into by choice, once we have entered it that relationship constrains the choices we may make. The other core familial bond—the parent-child relationship—often is not optional to begin with, and surely must not be treated as optional after that. It imposes heavy obligations on everyone involved, and yet it plays a crucial role in forming us to be capable of freedom and choice.

In this sense, the institution of the family helps us see that institutions in general take shape around our needs and, if they are well shaped, can help turn those needs into capacities. They literally make virtues of necessities, and forge our weaknesses and vulnerabilities into strengths and capabilities. They are formative because they act on us directly, and they offer us a kind of character formation for which there is no substitute. There is no avoiding the need for moral formation through such direct habituation in the forms of life.

In the family, this often means habituation in the roles reserved for spouses, parents, children, grandparents, and other supportive relatives. That means the form and structure of the family are essential to its ability to serve a formative purpose.

This is not necessarily good news, because family structure is not an easy thing to build and sustain. In fact, for the past few generations, our society has had enormous trouble doing both. We are plainly living through a collapse of family forms. About four in ten American children are now born into a family with only one parent—generally a single mother working hard to provide the resources, the structure, and the love and support her children need. Meanwhile, marriage rates have fallen, and married couples have tended to have fewer children over time. This has meant that family life in America has fallen away from the traditional pattern of family structure. That has happened for the most part without the emergence of a new or different durable institutional structure for the family, so it has happened as a deformation and has therefore been a source of disorder and disadvantage in the lives of many millions of Americans.[2]

The model of the traditional family—a mother, a father, children, and an extended family around them—has always been a general norm more than a universal reality. It is important not because everyone has lived this way, but because even those who live otherwise (as, one way or another, a great many families always have) could implicitly resort to this model of the family as a baseline to understand what they possess and what they lack. Formation often involves patterning ourselves after what we seek to resemble, and the ideal of family built around parenthood rooted in a stable marriage has always served that role, even for many people whose lives are not so traditional.

It is precisely on this front that family life in America has been affected by the penetration of culture-war politics into every institutional crevice in our society. The family, because it unavoidably constrains personal choice and expressive individualism, has been turned into yet another arena for controversy in our multifront political and cultural struggle. The particular shape of the debates we have had—whatever one thinks about same-sex marriage, the rise of cohabitation, single parenthood, or any of the other family-formation controversies of recent decades—has often caused us to perceive an emphasis on the forms of families as an effort to deny recognition and legitimacy to some individuals. This has meant that the popular culture has recoiled from the importance of form in our understanding of family, so that we increasingly come to define family formlessly, or want to allow it to take any form that individuals choose.

This necessarily requires us also to attenuate our sense of the function of the family, or of its purpose. The family as an institution has gradually come to be understood less in terms of its form (and therefore its potential to serve as a formative influence on individuals) and more in terms of its chosen-ness (and therefore its potential to serve as a mode of expression and recognition for individual identities, preferences, and priorities). Thus, to a degree the family, too, becomes a kind of platform, a way of being recognized.

This cultural tendency has plainly been driven by a passion for inclusion, and has surely advanced that vital moral cause. It is far from nefarious, even where it has been detrimental, and it has by no means always been detrimental. But both by fanning intense controversy around marriage and family and by altering our expectations of both, this tendency has made it harder for us to understand the family as a formative institution and to approach our roles in our own families accordingly. Among other things, we have gradually come to treat the intense and nearly universal desire for family life more as a longing for recognition than as a hunger for order and structure, and that, too, has distorted our understanding of what our society and its members want and need.

In this respect, the winds of social change buffeting family life have resembled those that have affected many other institutions. Because the family is such a foundational institution, however, altered expectations of it must function as both causes and effects of the societal transformations we have been tracing. A diminished sense of the family as a formative and authoritative institution leaves us less prepared to approach other institutions with a disposition to be formed by them. And the loss of institutional habits up and down our social life—from government to the professions, the academy, the media, and more—leaves us more resistant to the sometimes burdensome demands of family life.

We face a crisis of family formation—evident especially in rates of single parenthood—but we have increasingly responded to that crisis by downplaying the significance of the family's form. This is a way of avoiding the problem rather than addressing it. And it is deeply connected to the larger escape from institutions we have been tracing. By minimizing the significance and necessity of formation of all sorts for our free society, we have confused ourselves about the nature of the problems we face.

The family, perhaps more than any institution, forms us by constraining us—by moving us to ask, "As a parent, as a spouse, is this what I should be doing?" That dutiful question, which compels us to see ourselves as more than individuals performing on a stage, is the practical manifestation of the formative power of institutional authority. Its waning is a sign of serious trouble.

It is not just in the family that such thinking appears to have waned. We have seen it wane throughout the institutions we have examined, and it is certainly waning in civic life as much as elsewhere. We can see it plainly, for example, in the contemporary struggles of American religion.

We are living through a period of change and challenge for institutional religion in America. The evidence of crisis is overwhelming. Trust in religious institutions is at its lowest since routine polling on such questions began some eight decades ago. Regular church attendance is also near a nadir. But deeper signs of trouble can be found within the circle of believers. What ails American religion is best understood not as the rise of secularism or of non-affiliation but as a decline in confidence.[3]

We could illustrate this by many examples, drawn from the life of almost any religious denomination in our vast and diverse country. There are many to point to in the contemporary experience of my own Jewish community, and of many other minority religious faiths throughout our society. But the challenge might be best illustrated by looking at the two largest religious groups in our country, Roman Catholics and Evangelical Protestants, each of which composes about a quarter of the American population. The size of these groups means that they contribute significantly to setting the tone for American religious life and that they contain enough internal variety to let us trace a few broad themes without pretending we can grasp the full picture.[4]

Catholicism and Evangelicalism present us with two distinct kinds of institutional crises: a form of corrosive insiderism and a form of corrosive outsiderism, respectively. What is more important, each has been undermined by a corruption of its traditional strength, rather than an aggravation of its traditional weaknesses.

On the one hand, the largest and most institutionalized of America's formal religious denominations—Roman Catholicism—has been living through a horrifying crisis of debasement of authority and dereliction of responsibility. Revelations of decades of child sexual abuse by priests throughout the country (and in many other parts of the world) launched the crisis in the early 2000s, but it has grown worse in the last few years amid evidence of a vast institutional cover-up. The latter has proven perhaps even more damaging than the former precisely because of the institutional character of authority within the Catholic Church.

The hideous crime and sin of child sexual abuse is, tragically, by no means confined to the Catholic Church or any other religious institution. Rates of abuse by Catholic priests appear to be comparable to those of abuse by clergy in other religious groups and by school teachers and others routinely trusted to spend time alone with children. This in no way diminishes the horror of the abuses involved, of course. But the Catholic Church has certainly paid a special price for the prevalence of abusers among its clergy because it is a uniquely institutionalized Christian denomination, and one that views its institutions as channels and receptacles of its distinct divine authority. The church teaches its faithful that its priestly agents and ecclesiastical hierarchy are deserving of exceptional trust and authority. When they prove unworthy of such trust, the damage to the church can be even greater than would already be the case in any scandal involving the abuse of children.[5]

It is especially so because the grave offense in this case was not limited to those who abused children. The larger institution—from the parochial and diocesan level, to the very highest reaches of the American church, and even to the Vatican—appears to have been aware of many instances of abuse and to have acted to protect the abusers and the church rather than the abused. The priest abuse scandal is therefore a clear instance of a failure to uphold institutional responsibilities. Everyone involved plainly failed to ask themselves what their unique positions demanded of them. The abusers were debased by their own disordered appetites, and their protectors were in many instances debased by a corrupted form of institutionalism itself, which valued the protection of those within the institution over the protection of those the institution is meant to serve.

This is a classic kind of institutional corruption—the corruption of the insider that amounts to oppression of the weak by the strong. It is why institutionalism often has a bad name, and why populists and anti-institutionalists of all sorts can so often find a ready audience for accusations of corruption against the powerful and the established. Sometimes we lose trust in our institutions simply because the people who populate them turn out not to be trustworthy.

This form of the crisis has turned the strength of Catholicism into its weakness. Trust in the institutional church is uniquely important to Catholicism. It enables the integrity of the larger whole to respond to the corruption of particular individuals. But when corruption appears to be dispersed throughout that larger whole, believers have few legitimate avenues of recourse around the hierarchy of the church, and the very solidity of Catholic institutions threatens to undo their legitimacy.

Catholicism, in America and beyond, has enormous moral and intellectual resources to draw upon in the work of recovering from this scandal, and it will surely do so over time. There is reason to think that generational change in the church will play an important role in such a recovery, both because the accusations of abuse and cover-up are mostly from decades ago, and so are directed at older priests and bishops, and because, in the Catholic Church as in much of the rest of American religion, members of the rising generation of active faithful appear at this point to be more orthodox and tradition minded than their elders. They seek to purify the church and its institutions and have taken the crisis seriously.

That there are causes for hope, however, does not diminish the severity of the challenge American Catholicism now confronts. For our purposes, it is important to see the underside of institutionalism that such a crisis makes apparent. The prerogatives claimed by confident institutions—including, especially, the authority to make decisions of immense importance in private—impose heavy burdens of responsibility on those involved in leading them. Betrayals of trust in such circumstances can be catastrophic.

The danger of corrosive insiderism is a key reason for the skepticism of institutions that has long prevailed in the American character and that is so powerfully evident in our culture today. Our institutions are in peril not just because they are under attack but also because they too often fail to live up to their obligations. The first fact that must be faced by anyone concerned about the populist assault on our establishments is that the populists are right about a lot. Cynicism about institutional power cannot be fully understood apart from the realities of the abuse of that power—in religious institutions just as in others.[6]

In fact, it is fair to say that such hostility toward insiderism—to the extent it has always been inherent in our culture—actually began in the religious arena and spread from there. The perception of broadly dispersed institutional corruption was key to what drove the Protestant break from Catholicism to begin with, in the era of the Reformation, and is at the root of the Protestant skepticism toward authoritative mediation between man and God.

But such skepticism of institutionalized authority yields problems of its own. The other face of the contemporary crisis of religious authority in America involves a dangerous escape from responsibility rooted in this very flight from mediation—and so is akin to what we find in many of the other institutions we have considered. It is less a crisis of insiderism, or of oppression of the weak by the strong, and more a crisis of outsiderism, or of a collapse of structure and responsibility.

Just as American Catholicism has encountered a dangerous loss of confidence in the formal authority that is so crucial to its strength, so are some of the most robust forms of American Protestantism now confronting grave dangers rooted in their own strengths, which are quite different. Protestant institutions sometimes recoil from conceiving of themselves as institutions at all, and prefer to empower individual leaders to serve as voices of personal witness rather than look to structures of authority to mediate between believers and the sacred truth. This is a great strength of Protestantism. It is inviting and attractive, it encourages a certain egalitarianism among believers, and it bespeaks an authenticity that appeals to souls in search of the divine. But it also means that communities of believers sometimes place themselves in the hands of individual spiritual leaders who are not equipped to grapple with the responsibility they shoulder, and that their institutions are all the more likely to lack a cohesive party of the church that will put first things first. In the kind of broader cultural environment we have been exploring in these pages, that leaves some Protestant churches vulnerable to a particular form of the transformation into a platform for cultural warfare.

As we have seen, our political institutions are home to both major factions of the culture war—Left and Right—and as such they often become arenas of reciprocal performative outrage. Our media and academic institutions are more commonly home to the party of the cultural Left, and so at times they are honed into arenas for aggression by that party. These institutions become platforms upon which the modes and vocabulary of professional and academic work might be directed at essentially political or culture-war aims, and where activism goes by the name of scholarship or journalism. Many of our most robust and energetic religious institutions, meanwhile, are more often home to the party of the cultural Right. At times they are transformed into arenas for counteraggression of the same sort, and become platforms upon which the modes and vocabulary of religious formation and evangelism are directed to essentially political aims, and activism goes by the name of fidelity or godliness. The people charged with these religious institutions, and those who populate them, sometimes seem to be defined as much by a common cultural and political identity as by the tenets of their common faith—again, as can be the case in the academy, journalism, and elsewhere. Celebrity culture has also reared its head in these precincts, just as we have seen in other institutions.

We can discern this phenomenon particularly among white Evangelical Protestants, who at this point form the mainstream of American Protestantism. Voting patterns among that group are tightly aligned with religious affiliation, and some prominent religious leaders regularly argue for a kind of equation of political interests and religious teachings.

This has been especially evident in support for Donald Trump among white Evangelicals, who have been his most loyal constituency. More than 80 percent of them voted for Trump in 2016. More than most of his voters, they have persisted in defending him not only when he advanced policies they supported but even when he evinced behaviors and attitudes they would normally detest. In late 2018, about two-thirds of white Catholics and white Mainline Protestants (including significant numbers of Trump voters and supporters) agreed with the view that Trump's behavior had "damaged the dignity of the presidency," but a majority of white Evangelicals disagreed. There is evidence that support for Trump caused these voters to alter their prior views about the relationship between politics and morality. When white Evangelicals were asked in 2011 whether "an elected official who commits an immoral act in their personal life can still behave ethically and fulfill their duties in their public and professional life," only 30 percent said this was possible. In October 2016, just before the presidential election and in the wake of some extraordinary revelations of misogyny and other immoral behavior by then candidate Trump, 72 percent of white Evangelicals answered the same question affirmatively.[7]

For many Evangelical voters, supporting Trump is of course the result of a traditional civic calculus: considering their options, weighing how different candidates might govern with regard to issues they care about, and choosing the one closest to their preferred views and policies. As conservative columnist Marc Thiessen put it in 2018, "Christian conservatives are judging Trump not by his faith, but by his works. And when it comes to life and liberty, his works are good."[8]

But many others, including some Evangelical leaders with real institutional standing, have gone much further and put the weight of their religious institutions behind the political cause of supporting Trump. Jerry Falwell Jr., a prominent Evangelical and president of Liberty University, argued in endorsing Trump in 2016 that, although Trump had his flaws, he was a vessel of a godly mission, just as "God called King David a man after God's own heart even though he was an adulterer and a murderer." Pastor David Jeremiah compared Trump's daughter and her husband to the biblical Joseph and Mary: "It's just like God to use a young Jewish couple to help Christians." In this telling, the case for Trump is religious and not just secular. It justifies setting aside the traditional attitude of Evangelicals toward politicians and public life.[9]

These are exceptions, but prominent ones. They do not mean that there has been no secular justification for Evangelical support of President Trump, or that prudential political judgments among Evangelical voters who feel threatened by the progressive cultural aggression overtaking many of our institutions must somehow be in tension with these voters' religious convictions. But they do show that some religious institutions have come to view their purpose through the lens of our wall-to-wall culture war and so function as platforms for political and cultural combat to an unusual degree in our time. Uncomfortable as it may be for some conservative Evangelicals to acknowledge, there is in some of today's Evangelicalism a kind of mirror image of the culture-war proclivities increasingly evident in many elite institutions. In response to similar pressures, we find similar deformations, which present similar problems.

In many instances, these threats to institutional integrity are rooted firmly in claims of unmediated individual authority. As Baylor University's Alan Jacobs has argued, claims like those cited above, that Donald Trump has been chosen by God, are generally grounded only in the authority of the individual asserting them. Jacobs cites, for example, pastor Jeremiah Johnson's claim that God had made known to him that Trump was being used in the service of a divine purpose. Such an assertion, Jacobs writes, is "not a proposition that can be evaluated by any standards that unbelievers can understand. It cannot even be evaluated by Christians skeptical that God has spoken in a unique way to Jeremiah Johnson. It is a private revelation that depends on a prior belief that Johnson is a faithful channel of the Holy Spirit." It is therefore an example not only of the transformation of religious authority into a vessel for political activism but also of the risks inherent in religious authority operating outside of institutional frameworks.[10]

In this arena, as in so many others, we find that the rise of platform institutions and celebrity culture are together undermining structures of responsibility. The rise of megastar pastors has raised the prospect of a genuine celebrity culture within American Christianity. Andy Crouch, a prominent Christian author and journalist, has been raising the alarm about this problem in recent years. The kind of power that charismatic religious leaders can exercise in the lives of their followers can create temptations to corruption, he notes. That problem is nothing new. "But it is compounded by something genuinely new: the phenomenon of celebrity," he argues. "Celebrity combines the old distance of power with what seems like its exact opposite—extraordinary intimacy, or at least a bewitching simulation of intimacy." He continues:

> It is the power of the one-shot (the face filling the frame), the close mic (the voice dropped to a lover's whisper), the memoir (the disclosures that had never been discussed with the author's pastor, parents, or sometimes even lover or spouse, before they were published), the tweet, the selfie, the insta, the snap. All of it gives us the ability to seem to know someone—without in fact knowing much about them at all, since in the end we know only what they, and the systems of power that grow up around them, choose for us to know.[11]

The result, Crouch suggests, is the fading of a sense of responsibility that traditional pastors have to their flocks, and the loss of institutional strictures built up around them to protect all involved against abuses of power. This points to a different form of the failure to ask that dutiful question: "What choices and behaviors are appropriate given my position?" The lure of celebrity lifts leaders out of their protective institutional constraints and puts them on display. Its immediacy—the directness and authenticity of its message—is among the great strengths that Protestantism offers as a path to the divine. But it also renders Protestant churches distinctly vulnerable to the lure of celebrity that is so powerful throughout our larger culture.

A growing number of thoughtful Evangelicals are aware of this danger and are working to address it. They are focused particularly on curtailing the temptations of celebrity through the imposition of rules of practice. Crouch, for instance, has become involved in the work of Praxis, a network that puts forward what it calls "a rule of life for redemptive entrepreneurs." The rule involves strictly observing the Sabbath and so refraining from work for one day a week; tithing to the poor; systematically disengaging from phones, tablets, and computers for set times; committing to daily prayer; consciously avoiding isolation; and pursuing community.[12]

Other Evangelical leaders and thinkers have offered up similar rules. Rules of this sort are, of course, the foundation of institutional frameworks, and are intended to establish clear forms for behavior. For clergy and parishioners, these guidelines not only constrain and shape their actions but inculcate habits to guard against the lure of celebrity and assorted escapes from responsibility. In a sense, they create layers of structured mediation and restraint between a leader and his or her followers. They cut against the conflation of immediacy and authenticity because they recognize how vulnerable such immediacy can render a community of people.[13]

The growing awareness of the problem of celebrity, and the emergence of creative efforts to address it, are very good signs for the future of American Evangelicalism. There are other good signs too: among Evangelicals, as among Catholics, younger committed believers tend to be intensely serious, generally orthodox, and well aware of the challenges they face in an increasingly secular culture (though, to be sure, younger Americans as a whole are less inclined to be traditional believers at all). But for all these signs of hope, there is no denying the depth of the problem.

Whether in the Catholic Church, among Evangelical Protestants, or in Mormonism, Judaism, or the many other religious communities experiencing similar crises of confidence and order, it is enormously important that the problems we have examined here are acknowledged and taken seriously. That some key people look for effective ways to act—that a party of the church, distinct from the parties to our political and cultural conflicts, forms from within—is absolutely crucial now, because religious institutions are particularly vital if our society is to address the problems we have been tracing.

Our crisis of isolation, division, and cultural conflict is in many respects a crisis of meaning and even a result of a religious hunger left unsated by a culture that has lost some of its access to a traditional vocabulary of sin and redemption. The very forms of our cultural conflicts—with accusations of wickedness, calls for redemptive deliverance, persecutions of heretics, and demands for purification—are an indication of such hunger. In other words, the "great awokening" sweeping some of our key institutions points to an opening for a new great awakening.[14]

Our religious institutions are most important not for reasons of civic utility—not because they are useful in addressing social problems and meeting public needs, although they are. Our religious institutions are important because they offer us access to the fullest truth about our world. The great variety of religious convictions in our diverse society means that our ecosystem of sects and churches is variegated too. For its believers, though, each faith serves the ultimate and highest purpose. To find the worldly forms of our faiths sheered by the same hurricane winds that have done so much harm to our secular institutions is therefore to appreciate the depth of the problem we face.

But it is also to perceive the possibility of real solutions. A recovery of institutional responsibility throughout our society would need to involve a kind of devotion, even submission, to institutional formation that is simply most likely to emerge from our experience of religious formation. A recovery of the ethic of community also stands the best chance of beginning in the kinds of communities that first form out of common religious convictions. Such communities offer a way out of the endless combat of our culture war. The fact is that an attractive community, which plainly provides a venue for genuine flourishing, can change minds far better than an argument can. A way of life can be persuasive, even when we seem unable to persuade each other of much. But such community requires healthy institutions that attract our loyalty and devotion.

Yet, it is precisely for their capacity to build morally cohesive and formative communities that our religious institutions have become increasingly controversial in contemporary America. The question at the heart of some of our most divisive cultural conflicts has been whether institutions that embody the religious convictions of their members, leaders, or owners will be permitted to embody those convictions when they are not shared by our society's cultural elites. Whether it's Mormon schools, Lutheran hospitals, Catholic adoption agencies, Evangelical-owned businesses, or countless other corporate institutions moved by a religious mission, the pervasive culture war now threatens the integrity of these essential forms of association, just when that integrity is most badly needed.

THE SAME IS TRUE BEYOND THE REALM OF RELIGION IN AMERICA, IN the broader civic sector. And by broadening the aperture, we can better understand the importance of the work that civic institutions do for our society—not just as a means of bringing people together but as a way to meet practical needs. This is a crucial distinction for any effort to understand the role of institutions in causing and in ameliorating the social crisis we confront.

A long-standing premise of the study of institutions, and indeed of sociology since its earliest days, is that, in the words of José Ortega y Gasset, "people do not come together to be together, they come together to do something together." Institutions take shape and endure because they serve practical purposes in people's lives—often what we would now think of as economic or political purposes, though at times also more of a spiritual, social, or cultural purpose. As we have seen, institutions also frequently serve a formative purpose: in the course of carrying out their core functions, they also shape the people within them to carry out those functions with integrity, to trust one another and respect themselves, and to become better men and women. But because this formative purpose is often ancillary, an institution cannot endure the loss of its primary purpose; it cannot function only as a forge of integrity. People generally cannot be counted on to join or reliably participate in the work of an institution out of a desire to improve themselves. We will join and participate only if doing so will serve a more practical and immediate goal in our lives, and we can hope that in the course of such participation we may also become better.[15]

This points toward one possible explanation for the dramatic explosion of alienation in parts of our society in recent decades. The kinds of interpersonal institutions that have helped many Americans to find a place and make connections have been made less necessary by a variety of changes in our economic and political order, and therefore have become less attractive and less significant. The development of our economy over the past half century has often achieved marked improvements in efficiency by removing human intermediaries. Automation and the rise of e-commerce have made it much easier to be a functional loner in America, and as a result fewer of those Americans on the margins of our social order have been drawn inward toward relationships of mutual dependence and connection. Meanwhile, the welfare state has grown to take on many of the tasks previously performed by family, church, and civil society. The institutions it has gradually replaced have become depopulated, and their fundamentally social functions have been left unfilled.

This is not to say that the expansion of government into the realm of social services has been unwarranted or ineffective. In many instances, the bureaucratization of social services has helped those services reach vastly more people, and in fairer and more equitable ways. And yet, the replacement of a local helping hand by a check in the mail from a distance has involved more than a change of address. It has meant that we are less dependent on sources of help (in the family and community) that might demand something of us in return, or might offer us a place and a connection. It has also meant that local civic and charitable groups, religious institutions, and fraternal organizations simply have less to do, and therefore fewer ways to attract people out of isolation and into community. Both the character of modern markets and the character of modern government have thus enervated our traditional mediating institutions.

These kinds of institutions and the connections they offer are still essential to building relationships and attachments, though. They are vital to our psychic well-being. But we cannot expect them to remain strong if that is all they do for us. As Robert Nisbet put it more than half a century ago,

> Family, local community, church, and the whole network of informal interpersonal relationships have ceased to play a determining role in our institutional systems of mutual aid, welfare, education, recreation, and economic production and distribution. Yet despite the loss of these manifest institutional functions, we continue to expect them to perform adequately the implicit psychological or symbolic functions in the life of the individual.[16]

This means that if we are to draw people into meaningful relations within mediating institutions, we must find ways to help those institutions matter again in practical terms. That would require, among other things, looking for ways to redirect those "systems of mutual aid, welfare, education" and other services through rather than around our civic institutions. By letting civic, communal, religious, and social institutions have a hand in providing help to those who need it, we can better tailor assistance while also drawing people into the public arena who would otherwise be isolated. There is no simple formula for doing this, but we should strive to inject into the provision of public services and social insurance a general inclination to work through local institutions.

Another implication of this difficulty is that we ought to look for opportunities to launch new locally focused civic enterprises directed to meeting practical needs that are going unmet. The early twentieth century saw an explosion of local institution-building intended to meet novel social demand. We, too, face new pressures and needs—like the need to retrain workers in mid-career or to teach English and civics to new immigrants—but we have not seen a commensurate rise in institution-building. So, as older and more familiar practical needs have come to be met at a distance by e-commerce or faceless bureaucracies, new and less familiar needs have so far not drawn Americans into spontaneously formed groups in large numbers. That has left a lot of us isolated, neither bonded nor bounded by strong institutions, and increasingly out of the habit of organizing.

Add to this the availability of vast social media platforms that provide us with the illusion of organizing, and you find even less energy and interest devoted to genuine social formation. The model of social media activism—by which an ephemeral show of numbers stands in for a durable show of organizational strength—has gradually come to crowd out a great deal of traditional social and political organizing. Even political protests, which once offered a way of demonstrating logistical prowess and an ability to pull together large bodies of voters, can now be organized by putting out a call on social media, and so offer no proof of an underlying organizational infrastructure. The past decade has seen the rise of pop-up protests, which can be massive and yet are evanescent and leave behind little of consequence.[17]

This is even more of a challenge for nonpolitical civic organizing. Oddly enough, the fact that pooling resources and getting attention has become easier in the age of the internet and social media has meant that civic action involves fewer durable institutions and less interpersonal cooperation. Less does not mean none, to be clear. American civic life still teems with organizations in many places. But this is less frequently the case in parts of the country where the civic fabric is most strained and where isolation and alienation are most intense—and not by coincidence.

This kind of problem can really only be addressed by reviving and building institutions that can meet our needs while also drawing us together. To participate in meaningful institutions at the level of the interpersonal—the civic and communal level, the level of the school, the church, and the union hall—is to understand ourselves as embedded in relationships of commitment, obligation, and responsibility and to grasp the privileges that such embeddedness provides. Seeing that, and thinking this way, is itself part of the answer to the social crisis our society confronts. It can help us understand the ways we belong and how connection makes us stronger, and can inject a sense of place and proportion into our social thought and action. Our failing to grasp these ways of belonging is one of the reasons we feel lonelier and weaker than the objective measures of our national well-being would suggest. Such institutions provide us with a set of human commitments, not just abstract ideas. We become moral agents through them.

THE SAME COULD BE SAID OF MANY OTHER KINDS OF INSTITUTIONS, which is precisely why they matter, and why the problems they face are so important to understand. Over these several chapters of examples, we have seen the variety of ways in which our institutions at every level of society have grown frail and how we have found ourselves pulled out of them.

These troubles plainly fall into a pattern. Breaking out of that destructive pattern requires us to see it in action, which is what we have sought to do by tracing these individual instances. But it will also require us to understand in a more integrated way what it is we are losing and how it might be preserved and renewed—to draw together some of the lessons learned from these examples.

PART III
A PATH TO RENEWAL

eight

THE CASE FOR COMMITMENT

OUR SOULS AND OUR INSTITUTIONS SHAPE EACH OTHER IN an ongoing way. This is both good news and bad. When they are flourishing, our institutions make us more decent and responsible—habituating us in exactly the sorts of virtues a free society requires. The exercise of these virtues, in turn, helps our institutions flourish. This is a virtuous cycle. But when they're flagging and degraded, our institutions fail to form us, or they deform us to be cynical, self-indulgent, or reckless—reinforcing exactly the vices that undermine a free society. The exercise of these vices then makes it harder for institutions to flourish. This is a vicious cycle.

We are plainly stuck in such a vicious cycle in some key areas of American life. But how can we break it? If the degradations of institutions and attitudes reinforce each other, then we can only really break the cycle by consciously changing our attitudes about the institutions we are part of, and by reforming those institutions to better form us. Perhaps above all, we have to see ourselves as insiders, possessed of advantages that are ours to enjoy only if we are willing to be shaped by the responsibilities that come with them.

This won't be easy. The fact is that we resist the strictures of institutionalism for some powerful reasons. We will only conquer that resistance if we can understand it and therefore also see more clearly what we have to gain by overcoming it.

JUST WHY ARE WE SO RELUCTANT TO THINK INSTITUTIONALLY? As noted at the outset of this inquiry, America has a long tradition of anti-institutionalism, rooted in our Protestant culture, our liberal individualism, and our cult of authenticity. These remain powerful influences on our thinking, but they are not the only reasons why the term "institutional" has a bad name with us. Any case for institutionalism has to take account of its serious downsides.

Some of these are historical in a more concrete sense. The institutions of American life have not always been the sources of our strengths. They have sometimes been the foundations of injustice and the enablers of organized abuses of power. The term "institutionalized racism," for instance, is not some kind of metaphor. It is a very real and unavoidable facet of the American experience, past and present, and is one reason why the suspicion of social power in our society naturally extends to a suspicion of some institutions.

Such suspicion extends well beyond race: institutions can serve as enablers of majoritarian tyranny of various sorts. National majorities crushing dissent, local majorities using public power, and even dominant groups within social, educational, economic, occupational, and civic institutions can easily become domineering in ways that threaten the freedoms of others. This is a problem that should worry every institutionalist.

Within some institutions, it doesn't even take a majority to be oppressive; a small elite group with significant authority and power can do enormous harm. This is a form of the familiar danger of insiderism and corruption. Our institutions embody our way of life, so when oppression of the weak by the strong is part of our way of life, it is often given form in oppressive social establishments. Recent years have offered no shortage of evidence.

Quite apart from any explicit corruption or any power of majorities, moreover, institutions are almost inherently restrictive of individual liberty in its simplest sense. So, they have also come to be identified in the minds of many Americans with cold conformism or heartless proceduralism. The term "institutional" can call to mind bureaucracy, and there is little we Americans hate more. Bureaucracy often connotes a kind of institution that privileges its form over its purpose—or strict adherence to hierarchy and rules over the goals and ideals in the name of which they are deployed. This is another kind of institutional corruption, another form of insiderism, and it's one to which large, distant institutions are particularly prone.[1]

These kinds of insiderism lead not only to explicit abuses of power but also to an arrogance of the powerful that constitutes another downside to assertive institutionalism: loyalty to institutions tends to validate and reinforce the social status quo and to encourage contempt for those who would challenge it. It is easy to claim that mere possession of the institutions is evidence of righteousness or rationality and to dismiss any challenge to that dominance—from populist political movements, excluded minorities, or unorthodox ways of thinking—as self-evidently illegitimate attacks upon the social order. This kind of elite contempt is powerfully evident in our politics now and has a lot to do with the crisis of legitimacy we confront.

It should not surprise us, therefore, that the reaction against such contempt (a reaction that is a powerful force on today's political Right) takes an anti-institutional tone. Nor can it be very surprising that movements organized to champion the interests of racial and ethnic minorities (which are powerful forces on today's Left) often resist institutional terms and concepts too. Least of all should it surprise us that the case against bureaucracy (which speaks powerfully to all with libertarian inclinations) often understands itself as a case for individuals against institutions.

All of this adds up to a politics that resists institutions—both on the large, national scale and, increasingly, on smaller, more local and personal scales. And yet the hollowing out of institutions, and the radical individualism it tends to encourage, only exacerbates these very problems. It creates larger distances between the general public and the elites who dominate most powerful institutions, and so it intensifies social alienation. It leaves us fighting abstract theoretical battles in the wide-open spaces of our political culture, rather than addressing concrete practical problems within institutions. It closes off avenues to reform and renewal, leaving us wondering how the springs of cohesion and social flourishing could ever be replenished.[2]

So, while all of these downsides of institutionalism should be warnings for us, they should not blind us to the upsides. They remind us that no good can be attained in this world without trade-offs. The disposition against strong institutions arose for serious reasons. The arguments for transparency and individualism emerged as correctives to excessively rigid and imperious institutionalism. Such worries are serious, and need to be heeded. But we have to see that transparency and individualism, too, involve serious trade-offs. Institutions can be terribly oppressive, and yet we cannot do without them.

It's true that institutions can reinforce the rule of the strong and privileged in our society; but it is also true that without functional institutions the weak have no hope of vindicating their rights. Our institutions have sometimes embodied oppression, but they sometimes embody our highest ideals. To defend institutions is not to defend the status quo, or the strong, or the privileged. Functional institutions are most important for people who don't have power or privilege.

And though our institutions can become cold and bureaucratic, they are essential to our acting on our warmest sentiments; without them we grow isolated, alienated, and disillusioned.

This is the irony we have repeatedly confronted: the failures of our institutions have led us to demand they be uprooted or demolished, but we cannot address those failures without renewing and rebuilding those very institutions. We are right to be fed up with our institutions sometimes, but we need them to be respectable and legitimate. It is right that anti-institutionalism should guide our reactions against the excesses of institutional strength, but our problems today are more like excesses of institutional weakness, and so they require recommitment and reform rather than resentment.

Such a recommitment to the integrity of our institutions doesn't offer a quick fix to our social problems. It offers hard solutions, but they are the only ones that can be had. Real institutionalism requires the actual practice of some very challenging virtues. It demands a lot of us, but it promises a lot too. The last several chapters have helped us see what we lose when we fail to think institutionally. But that is not the same as seeing what we gain when we do make the effort. When we lay out just what a revitalized institutionalism promises, we can't help but notice that it looks an awful lot like what our society is missing, and not by coincidence.

A COMPREHENSIVE ACCOUNTING OF WHAT OUR INSTITUTIONS DO FOR us would be practically endless. But the most significant benefits institutions provide might be broken down into just a few categories: they constrain and structure our activities; they embody our ideals in practice; they offer us an edifying path to belonging, social status, and recognition; and they help to legitimate authority. By examining each of these, we can unspool the case for investing ourselves in a revival of our institutions—and we can also see why that kind of revival could be achievable.

That our institutions empower us by constraining us is often the hardest thing to accept about them. Our freedom-loving nature chafes against such restrictions. But by setting some boundaries on what we can do and on what can be done to us, functional institutions give us a frame of reference to decide how to behave.

We have seen the power of such a perspective again and again in the last several chapters. It is what leads us to ask not just "What do I want?" but "How shall I act here, given my position?" Its power is not limited to institutions that are defined by a corporate or legal structure where roles are explicitly formalized. In fact, it may be most evident in the family. Marriage gives spouses roles that help them think about what behavior is and is not appropriate. The relations of parents and children do too. "I'm a parent now, so maybe I shouldn't behave this way"—that's a thought that every father or mother has probably had. It's a thought that makes us better precisely by constraining us.[3]

The same is true, to various degrees, of the roles that institutions give us in our work, in our communities, in education, in religious life—in every realm of human action and experience. By setting boundaries and constraining what we can do, they implicitly instruct us and so form our character. Is this how a police officer or a pastor or a student or a legal guardian should act here? That question tests us. It is a burden, and it is a source of strength.

Of course, people often fail such tests. We all do. But even then, by imposing the test in the first place and draping an extra layer of responsibility and obligation over our naked humanity, our institutions help to protect the weak and restrain the strong. When we see our social lives as mediated by institutions that structure appropriate ways to do what we do, we are more likely to act responsibly and to demand responsibility of others.

This sort of constraint and accountability often is not legally prescribed. It acts on us implicitly—and thus moves us to choose to behave responsibly. After all, in a free society, people cannot be coerced to act well. The constraints imposed by functional institutions therefore don't only empower us, they also liberate us—they make liberal freedom possible. And they help us to see that liberal freedom is not license. Rather, it is contained within forms and formalities given shape by institutions. It is made possible by a closing of the distance between what we should do and what we want to do.

These forms and boundaries protect us not simply by restraining people who might do us harm or reining us in when we might go too far. They also provide stable foundations for risk-taking—a solid, reliable backdrop of rules, expectations, and norms that allows us to try new things by limiting some of the dangers. This is why one consequence of our loss of faith in institutions is a pervasive sense of flux and insecurity that makes us feel like everything is constantly changing, yet also makes us afraid to change much of anything. It is one reason why we have seen less dynamism in our economy in recent decades. In the absence of stable institutional frameworks, we have more trouble innovating and adapting to change.

Institutions also provide us with structure—which we often badly need but rarely ask for. Such structure isn't just a set of restraints. It can take the form of process or procedure. Our institutions sometimes give us practical, step-by-step guidance on how to achieve what we want. They tell us what it takes to get a license, or earn a degree, or lodge a complaint, or build a career. Observing such processes at work also shapes our expectations and assumptions. It builds habits of order and peace. "Like most habits, democratic behavior develops slowly over time, through constant repetition," Yoni Appelbaum has written. Those habits reach well beyond the political world, into every kind of association and joint endeavor. They teach us how to turn goals into projects and ambition into action, and how to do it together.[4]

Sometimes this means that institutions help us deal with disagreement and find accommodations. Form and structure can be essential for engagement and communication. We have seen this, or the lack of it, in the realm of social media—much of which is premised on the assumption that direct and unmediated interaction will bring us together. It hasn't worked that way. More structured institutions can contain and channel disagreements, giving them pace and measure and a path toward resolution. They can also help us cooperate, which is no less challenging. By giving individuals distinct roles in relation to one another—in the family, in the workplace, in planning a church dinner or running a meeting or organizing a school trip—institutions help us turn intention into action together. They tell us where to focus our energy and effort.

This points to the peculiar fact that institutional structure helps us to organize more than our relationships with other people. It also helps to organize our own internal life, our thinking. This is in part because institutions help us slow things down. They engender patience by giving us reasons to believe persistence will pay off. Even more important, they establish forms and orders for decision-making—they can force us to obey rules we would rather ignore, to follow procedure, to make a budget, to hear out other opinions. These kinds of processes can mitigate our biases and weaknesses and compel us to consider other angles.

Functional institutions also help us think by extending our horizon of expectations and priorities. They help us avoid the scourge of short-termism that is so closely connected to the vices of our culture now. Short-termism is often a function of unstructured thinking, which leaves us adrift in the moment and unable to see beyond it. It contributes to what social scientists call "recency bias": the tendency to assign undue importance to what has just happened or is currently happening, losing perspective regarding both the past and the future. Our media culture is now an endless study in recency bias, as intense attention is directed to the latest outrage or calamity to the exclusion of all that came before it. We consumers of that media diet end up feeling like dogs in the park—completely distracted by every passing squirrel until the next one comes by. Short-termism is key both to the dominance of celebrity culture and to our inclination to think about our institutional roles performatively. It moves us to conceive of success in terms of winning the moment rather than pursuing even medium-term goals.

Such short-termism makes it difficult not only to plan, but also to worry properly. It is a peculiar dysfunction of contemporary politics, for instance, that we seem to be unable to worry about problems except by panicking about them. We cannot rouse ourselves to take challenges seriously unless we can persuade ourselves that they present immediate and utterly apocalyptic dangers. And so we can't be concerned about the gradual effects of industrialization on the climate unless we persuade ourselves that innocents will soon be drowning in the streets of the world's coastal cities. We can't worry about the implications of the federal budget deficit for future prosperity without insisting that we are at the very precipice of a Greek-style debt crisis that will make shirtless beggars of our children. We can't worry that Donald Trump is unfit for his office in ways that could degrade our constitutional system over time unless that means he is about to destroy our democracy and trample our freedoms.

This inability to worry without panicking makes it much harder for our politics to take the future seriously, consider trade-offs, and see the case for less-than-radical policy action. It is plainly a form of short-term thinking: we are unable to take up a problem that is less than immediately existential because we are unable to actually worry on behalf of the future. Healthier institutions—not only in politics but throughout our social life—help us to consider the future by embedding us in a set of longer-term practices and commitments and letting us see ourselves as parts of larger wholes.

But our institutions help us think in an even more profound way than that. They shape our minds as they shape our character. As the sociologist Mary Douglas put it in her 1986 book *How Institutions Think*, this process works in both directions: Institutions are, on the one hand, the result of the thought and work of many people over time, so they let us benefit from a great deal of "preconception" in the best sense. On the other hand, institutions define the universe of possibilities in which our thinking happens—the range of options among which our judgment helps us choose. We think of rationality as an individual capacity, but, as Douglas writes, "the individual's most elementary cognitive process depends on social institutions."[5]

For this very reason, a trusted institution can also help us overcome some of the limits of our individual rationality by letting us fall back on a reliable process, rather than taking on every question from scratch. This doesn't guarantee that we will make the smartest choices every time, but it gives us a shot at making them more often.

We can see this play out, for example, in the logic of our constitutional system. The Constitution doesn't require all-knowing citizens; a proper respect for its structure can overcome some effects of ignorance and irrationality by requiring different sorts of institutions, answering to different constituencies and incentives, to cooperate and agree before a major governing decision can be made. Scholars of our democracy who constantly harp on the ignorance of the individual voter should think about this point: the answer to that ignorance is not to empower experts to rule over us; it's to allow the structure of our constitutional system—with its checks and balances and overlapping majorities and institutions—to guide our government's decision-making.[6]

This is also the case with formalized processes of making consequential decisions in many other kinds of institutions—decisions about hiring and firing, spending, building, and otherwise doing our work throughout society. In this sense, in a functional institution, what is required for good judgment is integrity more than a high IQ. Institutions can allow us to substitute character for calculation. In their absence, we have to substitute calculation for character—which often doesn't end well.

THIS TURN TOWARD THE POWER OF INTEGRITY BEGINS TO POINT US away from the purely functional appeal of healthy institutions and toward their even more significant advantages as social forms. Simply put, institutions embody our ideals, allowing us to meaningfully devote ourselves to them.

In a sense, all institutions are aspirational, because each exists to combine the actions of people within it to achieve a common aim. Some of these purposes might be higher or nobler than others, some are more mundane and banal, some could even be low and corrupt. But all serve as defining missions, and institutions are, in one way or another, distinguished by the ideals they pursue.

Those ideals are almost never completely realized, of course, even in the best of cases. But they give us a standard against which to measure the work of an institution and by which to direct improvements. Is this university a home for the honest pursuit of the truth? Is this church spreading the word of God and serving the least among us? Is this bank protecting its customers' deposits and getting them a good return? Does that store sell what I need at a good price? Is our family giving our kids the love and rearing they require? These ideals aren't all equally high and important, but each defines an institution. Institutions thus give us something to judge.[7]

And they often also give us something to love. By serving our ideals, institutions inspire loyalty and commitment. They come to stand in for what they provide, and so when they provide something we value highly, they can become objects of idealism and attachment that might otherwise be loose or unfocused. We are loyal to our team and our school and our profession not just because they are ours but because they come to represent something we value together. This kind of loyalty is in short supply in our national life now, and that is part of why we have seen an explosion of identity politics across the political spectrum. But identity politics is a shabby substitute. Institutional loyalty can give rise to a powerful sense of identity and solidarity, rooted in moral ideals and longings rather than in racial, ethnic, or biological markers.[8]

Healthy institutions enjoy an even more profound advantage over our shallow identity politics. Traditionally, we have drawn our identities from the greater wholes we serve, from concrete action rather than abstract connection. This deeper sort of identity directs our moral longings. Identity politics appeals to so many in our universities and elsewhere today because it speaks to what has become the generally accepted shape of moral action—that is, it offers a platform for displays of affiliation with accepted opinions. But genuine service to a higher mission can give much more satisfying expression to those longings, in the healthier form of devotion rather than mere expression.

Our institutions let us build and embody our identities through practical action, which offers some hope for solidarity and unity in a time of division. The question of how, in our diverse society, people with different conceptions of citizenship might live together cannot really be answered in theory but only in practice, which means through and in institutions. Actual people working together for a common cause don't have to agree about everything. An institution, particularly one built around some form of service, can bring people together without resolving philosophical differences between them or bridging chasms of identity at any conceptual level. This has always been a great strength of American life. Our society could never really work in theory, but the strength and variety of our institutions has meant that it can work in practice. In this respect, it is precisely the idealism of our institutions that enables them to be functional.

The kind of loyalty this engenders can sometimes be a check on institutional corruption and excess, because it is a loyalty to an ideal underlying the work as much as to the people who populate or run the institution. Some insiders can call out corruption in a company, a party, or a church because they are more loyal to the mission than to the personnel. Genuine fidelity is not just firm attachment to some person or group. It is a posture of submission to something higher, which links us with others who are similarly devoted. Our liberal culture is loath to admit that we desire to submit in this way, but leaving that desire unrequited on a mass scale is terribly dangerous, as it leaves us open to the lure of extremisms of various sorts—be they political, religious, social, or cultural—or to the appeal of abject tribalism. Functional institutions that exist in the service of high ideals help to direct and structure our submission so that it is effective and responsible, and therefore meaningful.

For this to work, the relationship between ideals and institutions must be fairly explicit—in the case of the most idealistic institutions, it must be very explicit—and it must be widely understood and clearly sustained in practice. It requires a certain earnestness in our relations to these institutions, a willingness to put aside our cynicism and expose ourselves as genuine devotees with others. It requires us to belong, and to be seen to belong. In return, it allows us to persist in valuing honor and obligation, duty and responsibility. Breaking away from institutional commitments can seem like liberation, but it more often feels like isolation—cold and lonely and pointless, devoid of love and loyalty. We yearn for love and loyalty, which means that, even if we do not always know it, we yearn for structure.

This may seem like a hopelessly earnest way to think about most of the institutions we encounter in our lives. But each of us can probably think of some institutions, one at least, that we do (or we want to) regard this way. Those institutions are where we should direct our energy, time, and work.

By providing us with an experience of meaningful membership, this earnest attitude toward the institutions we take most seriously helps us practice the virtues of loyalty, solidarity, and fidelity, while giving us some experience in dealing with the darker sides of human relations—managing egos, settling disputes, prioritizing different people's preferences and points of view, and paving paths to forgiveness. To be formed in worthwhile institutions is to be socialized for peace and responsibility—the importance of which can hardly be overstated. And it is at the same time to be provided with an experience of membership essential to averting the kind of alienation that is now so rampant.[9]

To argue for institutions is to argue for structure, which is no easy task. But it is structure in the name of our highest ideals. This argument can help us grasp why we should want order and moderation in the life of our society, not as restraints but as enablers of what we yearn for most. There can be no case for institutions without this idealistic facet of their purpose. It is easy to fall into talking about institutions in terms of organizational categories and pure structural analyses. But often what matters most about them is what that sort of thinking leaves out: their mission, their ethic, their ends, their ideals. They are more than organizations. They embody our aspirations. They are the forms animated by the spirit of our society. They stand for something, so that, by acting through them, we can stand for something too.

EVEN AS THEY LET US STAND FOR SOMETHING, THOUGH, INSTITUTIONS also let us stand out. It would be easy to conclude from the points I have made here that institutions are fundamentally means of self-negation or of putting others before yourself. But that is not the case at all. Healthy institutions can help to satisfy our intense desire for membership and belonging, not just by giving us something bigger to be part of but also by giving us a part to play, and therefore a way to shine—to be known, noticed, and appreciated as individuals.

Most institutions—and not just at the familial, communal, or local level—are in effect small ponds in which individual members can be big fish. We can be known and appreciated, we can be missed when we are absent, we can take part in the sort of interpersonal politics that we all like to complain about but actually enjoy and need: office politics, club politics, church politics, school politics. Each institution provides a place where everybody knows your name, your quirks, and your strengths and weaknesses. The absence of such places in the lives of many Americans has a lot to do with the breakdown we see in parts of our national life. As some of our small ponds have disappeared or been drained out, the opportunities we have to be big fish have grown more scarce.

This leaves people with two options: give up on the desire for recognition, or pursue recognition in the big pond—that is, pursue some kind of celebrity. That's one reason why, as we have thought about our social crisis, we have again and again run into the idea of celebrity as the enemy of institutional integrity. Celebrity is one way people can channel their desire to be known when there are no convenient ways to satisfy it. But a celebrity, as we have seen, is someone known mostly just for being known. Within the bounds of a healthy institution, you can be known for more than that: You can be acknowledged for the part you play in making the larger whole a success. You can be appreciated for integrity and responsibility—loved for your virtues, and not just noticed but recognized. If you've ever attended a retirement party, you know what this kind of recognition can look like and how satisfying it can be.

Within an institution, in other words, there is a difference between notoriety and prominence. It is a difference defined by a commitment to the purpose of the institution and to the ideals it works to advance. An institution is therefore a way to channel our natural ambition for status toward constructive ends.

This relates directly to the most prominent pattern of institutional deformation we have examined in these pages: the change from mold to platform. It is by offering a constructive channel for our ambition for prominence that functional institutions can help us adopt a formative, rather than a performative, understanding of their proper purposes, and so of *our* proper purposes. By narrowing the confines of the arena in which we seek to be appreciated, institutions help us avoid the temptation to treat them as stages. By creating paths to recognition through service, and through the advancement of collective goals, institutions offer us a chance for appreciation rooted in respect and dignity, not just popularity.

Functional institutions thereby give us incentives to seek prominence within them rather than on top of them—and so to seek it by advancing their causes, embodying their particular kinds of integrity, being constrained by their scale and purpose, and taking on their form as ours. That's how a commitment to thinking institutionally can help us combat one of the toughest problems confronting our society.

IN FACT, THE SAME CAN BE SAID OF ALL OF THESE FACETS OF WHAT healthy institutions offer us. They are ways of taking on the particular social crisis of our time. Obviously the picture of institutions I have drawn here is stylized and idealized—it is meant to sketch out their potential, which they often fail to reach. But it is worth seeing what our institutions can do, because it helps us see what they could do better, and therefore what we could do better.

The potential of institutions speaks directly to the distinct and sometimes confusing problems that trouble our civic culture now.

By restraining and bounding us, institutions can provide for the forbearance and patience that are so lacking in our common life. By structuring our action and thought, they can provide us with stability and confidence and a place in the grand scheme of our society. By embodying our ideals, they can help satisfy our hunger for meaningful belonging and offer relief from the suffocating cynicism of a populist age. By giving us a constructive path to social status and recognition, they can answer the temptation to mistake notoriety for glory, celebrity for accomplishment, and vain performance for character-forming work.

Recognizing that institutions benefit us in all of these ways helps clarify the character and causes of the social crisis we confront. It shows us that we are suffering not from an excess but from an absence—that we need and lack what healthy institutions provide.

But the populist character of this cultural moment points us to one further, crucial service that healthy institutions provide. Our social crisis is a crisis of legitimacy, and without taking up the vexing question of legitimacy, we cannot hope to recommit to our core institutions. We are alienated from them because we have, in many cases, lost confidence in their claims to power and authority.

Healthy institutions legitimate such claims—they not only help us to accept them, they help them to be more valid and true. The solution to our loss of faith is not to make people trust the institutions we have as they are. It is to make those institutions more trustworthy. That, in turn, requires a transformation of attitudes among the people within them and especially the people who lead them.

That daunting challenge, too, can be best understood through the lens of what healthy institutions do. It is where our argument must ultimately point—toward the obstacles to institutional legitimacy today, and toward some ways of overcoming them.

nine

BEYOND MERITOCRACY

A T FIRST GLANCE, DEMOCRATIC SOCIETIES LIKE OURS SEEM like they should be least troubled by the demands of legitimacy. Their institutions wear their claims to valid authority on their sleeves. Elected governments derive their just powers from the consent of the governed. Cultural, social, and economic power also ultimately answers to citizen and consumer preferences—at least in general terms. No one asserts a right to rule by force, or thanks to some unquestionable birthright.

But in fact, it is precisely because democratic societies are grounded in egalitarian presumptions that they are constantly troubled, and sometimes intensely agitated, by concerns about legitimacy. The democratic ideal suggests that a free and equal society should have no privileged class to rule it, but in practice, every society has its elites, one way or another. "Elite" has become a kind of insult in our time, but the term almost describes a tautology: Whatever the rules for election to office or ascension to influence, power, and wealth, some people will rise and some will not. Those who do rise are society's elite, because they have risen. Attempts around the world to overcome this basic reality and level elites out of existence altogether have resulted only in gruesome abuses of power. The question, then, is how the elite is determined, selected, populated, and replenished. Who gets the privileges of power and status, and on what grounds?

Elites in democratic societies are always under pressure to prove that the answers to these questions are sufficient, and so that they are worthy of authority and special standing. They have to believe this themselves, or else they will be racked by a debilitating guilt that could eat away their sense of purpose. They have to persuade others of this as well, or else their power will be a constant provocation to cynicism, alienation, and self-righteous populist upheaval. The two phenomena often go together: an elite enervated by self-doubt, outwardly smug but inwardly guilt ridden, is the other side of the coin of an alienated and indignant democratic public, outwardly contemptuous of all establishments, but inwardly starving for legitimate authority. The combination of the two, a combination we know all too well in contemporary America, amounts to a crisis of legitimacy.

The effects of such a crisis go well beyond a simple disrespect for those in power, or even anger at the unfairness of the privileges they have. This mix of guilt and resentment creates a sense of distance between elites and the public, which in turn leads citizens to feel that their leaders look down upon their way of life. It also fuels a perception that the rules of American life are rigged against the many for the benefit of a privileged few. All of this contributes to the alienation that pervades contemporary social life, discourages people from participation and engagement, and fuels outrage.

In other words, the impression that power and wealth are distributed according to an unjust standard is poisonous to solidarity and civic unity. As Irving Kristol pointed out in 1970, a democratic society is held together by more than just fair elections and free markets. "The results of the political process and of the exercise of individual freedom—the distribution of power, privilege, and property—must also be seen as in some profound sense expressive of the values that govern the lives of individuals," he wrote. If elites hold power or privilege for reasons that most of their fellow citizens don't consider genuinely meritorious, the entire society will lose respect for the rules it says it lives by. No one can enjoy living in such a society. It would feel not only unequal but unfree. "People feel free when they subscribe to a prevailing social philosophy; they feel unfree when the prevailing social philosophy is unpersuasive; and the existence of constitutions or laws or judiciaries have precious little to do with these basic feelings," Kristol concluded. The principles according to which our elite is populated and replenished must somehow be, as he put it, *persuasive*.[1]

When we fail to find such a persuasive justification for the privileges of an elite, the tendency of a democratic public is to rebel against that elite—to reject its claims to authority by lashing out against its use of power and demanding that the establishment be torn down. But populists are not anarchists. They demand liberation from oppressive authority because they want legitimate authority.

This creates a strange kind of problem in a democracy. Our politics seeks to give people what they ask for. So, in a time when what people ask for is distinctly different from what they want, politics tends to be unusually aggravating. This is not only because we aren't getting what we desire, but also because what we *are* getting intensifies that desire. Today, we ask for a politics of breaking down authority when what we really want is more respectable authority. When our politics challenges the establishment, it only sharpens our sense of what we're missing.

We can see this in the peculiar appeal of various kinds of confident claims to authority that are extrinsic to our politics right now—like the attraction of some younger Americans to streams of orthodox religion that reject liberal political ideals and to some secular moralisms that unabashedly demand self-discipline. We can see it, too, in the appeal of an identity politics that, for all its faults, draws clear lines between oppressors and oppressed. The attractiveness of these doctrines should tell us something about what we actually want from our politics, which is something very different from the antinomianism it is increasingly offering us.[2]

All of this is made worse in our time by an elite politics that responds to the populist demand to demolish authority by simply defending the status quo. This easily becomes an ugly cycle: frustrated voters want more legitimate authority yet demand the demolition of authority, and they are answered with a doubling down on what they perceive to be illegitimate authority. This creates a situation in which everyone can manage to be smug, wrong, and frustrated simultaneously. The effects are apparent well beyond politics. Frustration with elite claims to authority drives a loss of confidence in professionalism and expertise, particularly when experts insist on deploying their authority as a weapon in the culture war.

Any effort to address this escalating frustration should naturally point us back to institutions, because, whether we see it or not in the midst of our daily aggravations, elite authority is unavoidably channeled through elite institutions. This is why populist frustration with elite authority is so often expressed as a loss of faith in institutions. And it is why reconsidering our expectations of institutions, while reforming them to better live up to those expectations, could help assuage our crisis of legitimacy.

More functional elite institutions could do precisely what today's elite requires: constrain, direct, and form authority in ways better suited to persuading people of its legitimacy. Institutions can do this not by serving our elites, but by forming them to serve the broader public.

The alternative to corrupt elite institutions, then, is not anti-institutional populism but better elite institutions. We cannot do without such institutions, and so we need to invest our energies not in tearing them down but in building them up and reforming them.

Some institutions really are corrupt and broken, and to respond to their brokenness in a spirit of repair, rather than reprisal, seems unnatural. Yet it is essential. It may be the only way to take up the challenge of legitimacy that now confronts us everywhere.

To see how this might be achieved, we should notice something about how our crisis of legitimacy is connected to the other trends we have been tracing. The gradual transformation of our expectations of institutions—from seeing them as molds of character to seeing them as platforms for performance—has expanded the freedom of action of America's political, cultural, and economic elites. That has intensified the suspicion and mistrust that the larger public harbors toward these powerful people.

Institutions understood as formative are inherently constraining. They provide the people in them with boundaries and procedures, a code of behavior, standards of integrity, and formal responsibilities that help direct their ambitions and abilities toward a broadly shared purpose. In other words, they have the potential to humble and restrain our elites in the process of empowering them. They can offer frameworks for legitimacy. Institutions understood as performative, on the other hand, only further hone an already aggravating sense of entitlement. They provide prominent platforms for people with power, but they do not necessarily establish restraints. They therefore do not offer ways to make authority more legitimate.

Elites can establish their legitimacy in two ways, which generally must be combined: by making sure opportunities are available for others to rise into the elite and by using their own power and privilege with restraint and for the greater good. These are both challenging in a democratic society. For much of American history, the first of these requisites for elite legitimacy was the more obviously lacking. Through the middle of the twentieth century, the apex of American political, cultural, and economic power was largely the preserve of a fairly narrow white, Anglo-Saxon, and Protestant near-aristocracy centered in the Northeast. I say near-aristocracy because paths to power and wealth have always been more open in America than in most European societies. The ideal of the self-made man is rooted in some reality (especially in business and culture)—and even to the degree that it is a myth, it is a distinctly American one in a way that matters. But, though opportunities existed, rising to the greatest heights of American life has never been easy for those who did not start high.

These near-aristocrats were known as WASPs, though of course only a small sliver of America's white, Anglo-Saxon Protestants composed this aristocracy. They were raised to rule and exercised extraordinary power in some key American institutions. Their claim to power, like that of most modern aristocracies, was a mix of heritage and rearing. They possessed their privileges by virtue of their birth, but they were raised and educated in ways intended to prepare them for responsibility and authority. They were—at least in principle, though in many cases very much in practice—expected to subject themselves to a code of behavior, a commitment to public service, a degree of personal reticence, a regard for the rules of fair play, and a sense of responsibility rooted in the implicit recognition that their power was an inherited privilege, not an earned achievement.

Obviously even the limited moral code of this noblesse oblige never lived up to its ideals. The WASPs, like any elite, were frequently arrogant, entitled, and guilty of abuses of power. But they often internalized and institutionalized their code of behavior such that these abuses were also hypocrisies, and this did restrain, form, and direct the behavior of American elites. Their faults were many, but these near-aristocrats also achieved a lot, right through the era of the construction of America's mid-century institutions—in response to the Great Depression, the Second World War, and the emergence of the Cold War. Such institutions, throughout their many years of dominance, were the WASPs' other claim to power, and particularly to political power. They governed boldly and, in some crucial cases, successfully.

But by the middle of the twentieth century, it was becoming clear that these claims to power could not remain persuasive as our culture became ever more liberal and democratic. The WASPs were undone by the exclusive nature of the criteria for entrance into their elite— which largely excluded those not born into a narrow Northeastern gentry and almost entirely excluded Catholics, Jews, women, and racial minorities. Such discrimination not only became untenable in a society growing more inclusive and diverse but also became intolerable to much of the WASP elite, which gradually lost its sense of legitimacy and became persuaded that its institutions would need to open themselves to outsiders and adopt new criteria for ascent to the heights of American life.

In line with the democratizing spirit of the age, these criteria had to somehow avoid special favor and privilege. This meant, almost ineluctably, elevating an elite whose membership was determined by some measure of ability or intellect. The idea was hardly novel. It had been the organizing principle of the professional civil services that had taken shape throughout the West in the nineteenth century, and in some respects it reached back to Confucian China, if not earlier. Some set of exams, which might be relied upon to offer relatively objective measures of relevant abilities, would serve to filter potential elites. Those who scored high enough would be set on a path toward authority and privilege. Such filtering would take no account of family background, sex, race, religion, ethnicity, or other such characteristics. All that would matter would be a measure of merit. And thus was born the meritocracy.

THE TERM "MERITOCRACY" IS GENERALLY ATTRIBUTED TO MICHAEL Young, a British intellectual (and Labour Party member of Parliament) who coined it in the title of his 1958 book *The Rise of the Meritocracy*. The book was a work of fictional social commentary, and the term was intended to be pejorative. The book takes the form of a history of British social evolution supposedly written in 2034, which describes the replacement of Britain's aristocratic ruling classes by a caste of the best and brightest—as measured by tests of intelligence.

For Young, meritocracy was not the natural extension of democracy but a betrayal of it. "Today we frankly recognize that democracy can be no more than aspiration," his fictional narrator notes, so that society is ruled "not so much by the people as by the cleverest people." Young could clearly see that just finding a new way to select a narrow ruling class was not going to address concerns about the narrowness of that class—and that basing power and privilege on intellect could easily make things much worse. His book essentially describes a dystopia.[3]

But for reformers of America's elite institutions, many of them guilt-ridden WASPs, meritocracy did seem like an extension of democracy, because it involved broadening the criteria for joining the upper reaches of American life. Filtering for elites by testing for some objective measure of merit would create a much fairer upward path for anyone who showed ability, regardless of where he or she might come from. By the 1970s, meritocracy (employed without its original pejorative connotation) was in common parlance among American reformers, especially in higher education.

Because prestigious colleges are the King's Highway into every other elite institution, higher education has been at the center of meritocratic reforms from the start. Basing admission on standardized testing—especially the SAT, introduced in the 1920s but brought into wide use in the middle of the twentieth century—offered a way to select students from a relatively broad range of backgrounds. The appeal of the tests was not so much that they measured the skills or abilities most relevant to college success as that they measured those relevant skills and abilities that could be quantified without regard to an applicant's other characteristics. They offered a single, objective standard of comparison, and so would break the stranglehold of the patrician WASP families.

The new approach to admissions quickly allowed for more Catholic and Jewish students in elite universities—and later also for more students of Asian ancestry. Over time, and partly with the aid of affirmative-action formulas, they were soon joined by a greater number of African American and Hispanic students, while the integration of women into elite universities (largely in the 1960s and '70s) meant that these schools also stopped being boys' clubs. Although family-legacy admissions certainly continue, and the WASP lines are still overrepresented in elite schools, there is no doubt that today's American elite is far less narrowly drawn in terms of race, ethnicity, religion, and sex. This has opened opportunities for able Americans from many backgrounds and diversified our elite dramatically.

These elites of different backgrounds nonetheless do have one thing in common: they all measure up by the standards that are now said to represent merit. Yet those standards are not by any means self-evidently suited to supplying us with an able and legitimate elite. And a merit-based system cannot avoid the simple and unchangeable fact that an elite is inherently narrow and exclusive.

In fact, our meritocracy has not even been able to avoid the tendency of elites to become outright aristocracies—that is, to transmit privilege generationally. Thanks to both assortative mating and the powerful incentives to game the tests that grant entry into the American elite, children whose parents are in the upper echelons of our society have a very strong (and growing) chance of finding themselves in those upper echelons as adults.

Moving from the WASP near-aristocracy to our meritocracy vastly enlarged the pool of potential elites in America in the middle of the last century. But that really happened only once—or, rather, it happened for one generation. Since then, with each generation of meritocracy, the pool has not enlarged, and in some respects it even grows narrower and tighter. This process has both contributed to and been intensified by growing economic inequality over the past several decades. As William Deresiewicz has noted, the percentage of students at selective colleges whose families are in the top quarter of income earners in America has gone from roughly 45 percent in 1985 to more than 65 percent today. Our meritocracy is plainly rearranging itself into a more familiar aristocratic pattern, which leaves us less and less persuaded of its claim to legitimate authority.[4]

For similar reasons, the American elite has actually grown more homogenous in terms other than race, sex, ethnicity, and family connections. Business elites, professional elites, political elites, cultural elites, media elites, and academic elites were not so long ago quite distinct groups of people in American life—each with its characteristic set of educational backgrounds, cultural identities, political affiliations, and life experiences that crosscut in constructive ways. Today, we increasingly find a uniform body of elites atop these different institutions, all of whom share the same kinds of educational backgrounds, cultural affinities, and political priorities. Different sectors of American society no longer really have their own elites because there is just one elite, and it is increasingly becoming its own sector of society.

What is worse, this new aristocracy is in some important respects less reticent about its own legitimacy than the old. Because each of its members must work to prove his or her merit—to pass the key tests and clear the key hurdles—today's elite is more likely to believe it has earned its power and possesses it by right more than privilege. Because our elite as a whole has inclined to this view, it tends to impose fewer restraints on its use of authority and generally doesn't identify itself with the sort of code of conduct that past aristocracies have at least claimed to uphold. Even when today's elites devote themselves to public service, as many do, they tend not to see it as the fulfillment of an obligation to give back but rather as a demonstration of their own high-mindedness and merit.[5]

A meritocracy naturally assumes its authority is merited. But the idea at the core of our meritocracy is radically individualistic and dismally technocratic: merit is demonstrated by test scores and a glittering resume, rather than service to the larger society, and is then often put to use in various forms of management and administration. The sort of elite this produces implicitly substitutes a cold and sterile notion of intellect for a warm and spirited understanding of character as its measure of worth. Our society (including some elites) increasingly cannot escape the sense that this is an unjustifiable substitution. But, rather than impose tests of character on itself, our elite inclines to respond to these concerns with increasingly intense displays of its ideal of social justice. It doubles down on the logic of meritocracy, adopts the language of privilege in its critiques of the larger society, and pushes for even more inclusive criteria of admission to elite institutions—all in an effort to make its claims to authority more persuasive.

But these efforts miss a simple point. The claims to legitimacy of today's elite are being met with skepticism, not because it is too hard to enter the upper tier of American life (though it is), but because those in that tier seem to be permitted to do whatever they want. Our elite is increasingly guilt ridden, and the broader democratic public is increasingly cynical about its leaders, not so much because too few Americans can get into elite colleges as because those who do too often go on to exercise their power without restraints or standards.

Precisely because our elite does not think of itself as an aristocracy, it does not perceive itself to be in need of restraints. Ironically, to strengthen its case for legitimacy, it might have to understand itself more as an aristocracy. As the social critic Helen Andrews argues in an astute essay on this subject, "The meritocracy is hardening into an aristocracy—so let it. Every society in history has had an elite, and what is an aristocracy but an elite that has put some care into making itself presentable?"[6]

What would it mean, though, for our elite to make itself presentable or persuasive? It would surely require some sense of what has made it unpresentable or unpersuasive to begin with. Our meritocracy has lacked that sense. We have implicitly mistaken an idea of merit meant to broaden the entry criteria into elite institutions for an idea of merit that could justify and legitimate authority. But authority is not legitimated merely by the ways it is obtained. Often more important are the ways in which it is used.

So, to address our crisis of legitimacy, it does make sense to look for ways to broaden the upward paths in American society—to make sure power and privilege are afforded on more fair and equal terms. But we will need to do more than that. Opening pathways into the elite and making them fairer cannot be an excuse to let our elites use their power without restraint or accountability. The WASP gentry was wrong to close the doors of their powerful institutions to women and religious, racial, and ethnic minorities. But they were not wrong to impose a demanding code of conduct and restraint on those within their institutions. Our elite, however it is formed, requires such restraints and obligations too. As we think about how the meritocracy might be made less obnoxious, we will also need to think about how to respond to the fact that it is, in some respects, unavoidably aristocratic. We will need a code of conduct to which we all might be able to hold one another, but that can be applied especially to people in positions of authority and privilege. We will need ways of making sure, in public, that people in power are constrained by responsibilities and duties.

What forms could such a code of conduct take in our time, though? And how could it possibly be imposed? Those crucial questions take us back to the core argument we have been tracing in these pages and help us to see how that argument might address the social crisis that torments our society.

THE RECKLESS ARROGANCE OF AN UNCHECKED ELITE CANNOT BE humbled by formal restraints alone. And the reckless resentment of an alienated public cannot be remedied by procedural assurances. Both require higher common ideals to which they might be drawn.

Our meritocracy implicitly substitutes intellect for character and efficiency for integrity. This makes for an inherently distasteful attitude among the powerful, but it becomes downright intolerable when our leaders seem to be not even particularly brilliant or effective. In those times—these times—in particular, the broader public is forced to ask why it should take elite claims to authority seriously. Why should we trust our institutions and those who run them?

That question has been with us from the start of this inquiry. The basic answer should be clearer in light of what we have learned. We trust our institutions when they form the people in them to be more worthy of trust and provide everyone else with standards by which to judge those people. But in recent decades we have watched our institutions gradually lose sight of the importance of that function and instead begin to serve merely as platforms upon which individuals can perform. To regain our trust, the people who populate our institutions would need to understand themselves through those institutions again, to see their roles and characters as formed by them. That would take both institutional reform and a change of attitudes geared toward a recovery of the formative, and thus constraining, purpose of key social institutions.

The kind of institutionalism that would revitalize Congress, the university, the media, churches, and families would also contribute mightily to the capacity of those institutions to engender trust and legitimacy. The duty-laden institutional question—"Given my position here, how should I behave?"—is precisely the question our elites (like all Americans) will need to ask and answer persuasively if they are to make a strong claim to authority.

But that kind of question is a challenge to the logic of our meritocracy in much more than a merely formal sense. It is a question that implicitly assumes a different standard of merit and, in some respects, an altogether different conception of the human person—a more modest, less ambitious anthropology with much to teach us.

It is not a coincidence that a performative rather than formative understanding of institutions has arisen in our age of meritocracy. To see institutions as platforms for performance is to deny them their role as molds of character, and by extension to deny our very need for such formation. Our culture now often does deny that need. Both the libertarian and the progressive ideals of freedom assume a human person already fully formed, requiring only liberation from oppression of various sorts to be free. The meritocracy is rooted in an idea of achievement that tends to take the fact that someone has reached a position of privilege as evidence that this person warrants trust, or at least has paid his dues.

The vision of the human person underlying these assumptions is loaded with very high expectations of the individual, but it therefore makes only modest demands of institutions. Left to himself, the individual can exercise his capacities and pursue the good; our institutions need only to enable him—if not, indeed, to display or promote him.

But this vision has always been opposed in our traditions by a far more skeptical view, which assumes that a person begins imperfect and unformed—not to say fallen. This other ideal comes loaded with rather low expectations of the individual, but it therefore demands a lot of our institutions. It assumes that each of us is born deficient but capable of moral improvement, that such improvement happens soul by soul and so cannot be circumvented by social or political transformation, and that this improvement—the formation of character and virtue—is the foremost work of our society in every generation. To fail to engage in it is to regress to pre-civilizational barbarism. This work is the essential, defining purpose of our institutions, which must therefore be fundamentally formative.

This more skeptical vision of the human person and the purpose of society's institutions has roots that run deep in Western civilization, but it is now very controversial. The assault upon formative institutions in our time has everything to do with just how controversial it has become. It is why we find battles raging around every one of the core formative institutions of our society, including family, faith, work, community, education, and our republican form of government. It helps explain the very shape of our culture wars.

Part of the reason this view is so controversial is that it suggests that the fundamental or primary problem in a society like ours is not the oppression of the weak by the strong but the fragility of the preconditions for social order and freedom. If, as Jean-Jacques Rousseau famously put it, "man is born free, but everywhere he is in chains," and if those chains are more or less society's oppressive social institutions that deny most human beings their rights and liberties in the service of a select few, then we can make a better world by standing up for the weak against the strong and breaking those chains. But if instead man is born broken and everywhere he is made more whole by society's institutions, then the best way to improve the lot of those in need is to reinforce our institutions and enable more people to benefit from them. Of course, both are true at the same time: we all require formation, and the weak are often oppressed by the strong. But which is the primary problem? Which would need to be taken on first in order to enable us to address the other?[7]

It can almost be said that the answer each of us would offer to that question determines the side of the contemporary culture war on which we find ourselves. At the very least, it tells us a lot about where we fall along the traditional Left/Right axis that (broadly speaking) has given form to liberal politics for centuries. And it has a lot to do with our attitude toward the meritocracy—which after all embodies a form of the idea that our merit is there to be measured and that granting privilege and power to those who measure up, regardless of where they come from, is a way of treating everyone fairly. This is one important reason why our most meritocratic institutions tend to fall on the Left side of the culture war.

This divide is also, finally, an important reason why those meritocratic institutions now face a deep crisis of legitimacy. They demand too little of the people they empower, because they expect too much of them. Our meritocratic institutions, including those that are explicitly educational, evince the view that their purpose is to elevate the people in them far more than to shape them—to let them be who they are, rather than to make them who they ought to be. As a result, they fail to demand, and therefore produce, integrity and reliability. Their claims to authority are inherently unpersuasive to the larger society.

Such claims would be much more persuasive if they were rooted in an institutional ethic that promised restraint, formation, and responsibility, and so that set about advancing clearly defined institutional goals in ways explicitly intended to demonstrate trustworthiness. This would mean subsuming individual ambition in institutional ambition and directing it accordingly. It would mean enabling and expecting the people who populate key institutions in our politics, economy, and culture to pursue status and prominence within those institutions—by advancing their aims and embodying their ethics—rather than in the vast open space of the larger society by standing atop the institutions and yelling. And it would mean understanding each institution as giving its participants a place, a role, and a set of relationships rooted in their need for formation.

The way to take on the crisis of legitimacy we now confront, in other words, is to reinvest ourselves in our institutions—to work to reform them with integrity in mind and, at the same time, to pour ourselves into them and so let them form us. This would mean allowing the ethics of our institutions to be shaped a little more by the instincts of the more conservative party to our contemporary culture war, not to the exclusion of the more progressive party, but rather in pursuit of a more durable balance—with the aim of containing the conflict and preventing it from flooding and drowning our national life.[8]

In a sense, as we saw when considering the clashes in our universities, the two sides of the culture war seek to remind the larger society of something it takes for granted. The Left wants to remind us of the injustices we have ignored—of some of the ways in which the weak are trampled by the strong in our society, while everyone else walks by without stopping to help. If we are forced to see these injustices, progressives contend, we will not be so content with the status quo and might take up essential struggles on behalf of the vulnerable. To overlook these injustices is to live a morally callous existence and to be unworthy of all that we have. The Right wants to remind us of the preconditions for flourishing that we take for granted—all of the ways in which our modern, liberal civilization (including our pre-liberal religious and moral traditions, the rule of law, markets, and norms of pluralism) has immeasurably improved the lives of countless millions and makes it possible for so many of us to benefit from its advantages. If we are forced to see these preconditions for thriving and to realize how little we would have without them, we will be more inclined to reinforce and defend them. To take them for granted would be to live ungratefully and risk losing humanity's greatest achievements.

A great deal of our politics consists of the failure of partisans of each of these views to grasp what the other is getting at. In debates about some of the most heated controversies we confront (like immigration, policing, and civic education, among many others) one side tends to think the issue is whether oppression of the weak by the strong should matter and the other assumes the question is whether the preconditions for civilized social order are important. The two sides argue past each other, but each thinks the other is offering an immoral and irresponsible answer to a critical question, and the result is intense mutual animosity.

There are some sets of issues, however, regarding which one side simply must learn something from the other—whether because the power of the other's argument is overwhelming as a practical matter or because the problem our society confronts in that arena demands to be understood a certain way. This seems to me to be true, for instance, around questions of race in American life, where the Right simply must make a more concerted effort to grasp more of what is true about the point the Left is advancing. And it is true, I think, with regard to the condition and purpose of our institutions, where we can hardly hope for any progress unless the Left grasps more of what is true about the Right's approach.

This becomes especially clear when we consider the reasons behind the crisis of elite legitimacy that our society confronts now. The recovery of a formative idea of institutions is essential to the revival of legitimate authority, without which the future of our free society is at risk. The lessons we can learn by investigating that crisis point beyond themselves, however, to a broader teaching about the nature, purpose, and troubling evolution of our institutions, and therefore also about the preconditions for the American renewal we all want.

CONCLUSION

A MERICANS ARE HUNGRY FOR HOPE AND RENEWAL. ALL OF us, on every side of all political divides, are increasingly aware that the status quo is not sustainable. We have seen horrendous failures of responsibility, not only among people we disagree with but also among those we would like to be able to count on. Abuses of power—whether in Hollywood or Washington, the Catholic Church or the university—are beginning to compel some real moments of reckoning. The sheer unpleasantness of our political culture is driving a revulsion that has only begun to take shape. An increasing awareness of the distorting effects of information technology and social media on our minds and our relationships seems on the verge of launching a reaction too.

Some common denominators among these excesses—like the risks of celebrity culture, the danger of unrestrained cynicism, the costs of irresponsibility, and a mounting crisis of legitimacy—should compel us to think hard about what we must demand of our institutions. Again and again, institutional failures seem tied to the emergence of a performative ethic over a formative one. Institutions that understand themselves as interchangeable platforms cannot hold those within them accountable to each other or to an ideal held in common, and instead they enable individuals to avoid responsibility and behave anti-socially. They encourage an outsiderism that is poisonous to solidarity and legitimacy. They discourage any sense of ownership and obligation. And this, in turn, creates social vacuums, which are painfully evident all around us.

We are all tempted at first to conclude that only outsiders can save us. This is why so much of the energy of our politics is spent tearing down supposedly powerful establishments. The fact is, though, that we do not need more outsiders who pretend they are just critics with no power to act. We need more insiders—institutionalists who will be earnest both in their efforts to build frameworks for common action and in their acceptance of the duties that accompany power.

Those in our society who have the most power—our leaders and elites—especially need to resist the urge to pretend they are outsiders. But everyone else does too. Instead, we must all accept the responsibilities that come with the positions we hold, and we must ensure that obligations and restraints actually protect and empower us. We need to inhabit these institutions, love them, and reform them to help make them more lovely to others as well.

In one arena after another, we face the challenge of drawing alienated people back into our institutions. We can point to all kinds of complicated theories about how to build the trust required to accomplish this. But the simplest way is for the people who inhabit our institutions—that is, all of us—to be more trustworthy. We can each work at that.

This might seem like an awfully modest response to the immense social problems with which our inquiry began. That is because it is at best a partial solution. But it is also because taking some modest steps together, particularly when they involve thinking differently about ourselves and our roles, can truly make a difference.

That is why the case advanced in these pages may be more than wishful thinking. If the problem we face, or a significant part of it, is that we have stopped thinking of ourselves as formed and molded by the institutions that surround us, then one key to improving things would be a change of mind-set and expectations. We don't have to figure out how everyone might do this; we just have to do it ourselves. You and I. We can do it in small ways—in thinking about how to use our time and energy, how to pursue our goals, how to judge success and failure, how to identify ourselves when people ask us who we are, how to measure our responsibilities. Approaching the social crisis of our time through the lens of institutions gives us all something to do by giving us *each* something to do. It doesn't require some universal social movement or a public policy agenda or a religious revival. These might all be long-term hopes. They are all needed. But the scope and scale they would require should not paralyze us, because there is something small we can do to start.

Many Americans are not lucky enough to have the benefit of a flourishing family, or the opportunity for rewarding work, or an uplifting education, or a thriving community, or a humbling faith, let alone all of these at once. But some combination of these soul-forming institutions is within the reach of most, and the work of reinforcing them, sustaining the space for them, and putting them within the reach of as many of our fellow citizens as possible is among our highest and most pressing civic callings. All of these institutions now need us, and we can help by taking them seriously.

We can give them our time and effort. We can give them our identity and our self-consciousness. We can understand ourselves as defined by the institutions that matter most to us. We can judge ourselves by their standards, hold ourselves up to their ideals, take seriously their forms of integrity, and align our pride and ambition with theirs. We can serve them by reforming them to make them better able to achieve their potential. And we can serve through them. We can yearn not for the formless autonomy of the independent contractor but for the rootedness and responsibility of the member and the partner and the worker and the owner and the citizen.

There is a word for attitudes like this. The word is devotion. What's required of each of us is devotion to the work we do with others in the service of a common aspiration, and therefore devotion to the institutions we compose and inhabit. That kind of devotion calls for sacrifice and commitment. It calls on each of us to pledge ourselves to an institution we belong to unabashedly. To abandon ironic distance and dispassionate analysis and jump in. Even to submit to its demands on us. This kind of devotion is not only necessary, it is actually very attractive just now. We want objects of devotion, we want something to commit to.

Younger Americans especially seem hungry for these kinds of callings. But they often don't see that what they seek is already within their reach. They are confronted mostly with models of dissent and rejection. Even many of our traditionalists are dissenters—wondering out loud if their inheritance is just a burden, and if maybe our way of life has failed. We lack a grammar and vocabulary for articulating what we are for. It's easy to be fashionable rebels. It's harder to remind ourselves why our core commitments are worthwhile. That is the kind of case that institutionalism now involves, and why it is so crucial.

Dissent and complaint have their place, of course. But in a twilight age, a time of exhaustion and corruption, we need to understand that making complaint our common parlance and criticism our permanent stance can be deeply corrosive. It encourages an ethic of gleeful demolition and self-indulgent gloom. It makes it hard to practice devotion and to pursue a meaningful renewal.

There is reason to think that renewal is possible, because the hunger for it is evident in the very symptoms of decline around us now. The fact of our dissatisfaction should send us searching for signs of that hunger. But these signs might not be quite what we expect. They might at first look like a hard-edged student movement demanding conformity, when what the activists are really seeking is legitimate authority. Or they might look like young people flocking to teachers of discipline and order as a first step on a search for meaning or for God. They might sound like communities angry at generations of mistreatment by law enforcement reaching at first for a vocabulary of resistance and rejection but ultimately yearning for inclusion, equal justice, and belonging. They might come in the guise of a populism that insists it sees corruption in all directions but is ultimately desperate for an integrity that it can barely name. As demand can drive supply, so can social failure yield to resurgence and renewal—if we are open-minded about the forms that this demand might take.

To be able to spot this hunger and yearning, we do need some idea of what we are looking for. Or rather, we must consider what some angry and dejected fellow citizens might want but will not ask for by name. This is why we need to train our senses to perceive and grasp what institutions do. Because institutions are what everyone is talking about but no one names. They are at the core of what we lack, but we often see through them as though they were invisible and so we too rarely rush to repair them when they're broken. They are at the heart of our achievement as a society, but our theories of ourselves—the political and social philosophies that claim to describe American life—are all far shallower and more crude than our reality.

This often means we are blind to the resources at our disposal to help spark the resurgence we want. It's true that our commitments to institutions have been in decline for some time, but they have not gone away. A huge portion of how we live our lives amounts to endorsements of institutions. So we have a lot to work with, but doing that work will require us to make such endorsements a little more explicit and to understand what works in our society a little more clearly. It will require not only a sociology of misery and breakdown, which we have been getting pretty good at lately, but a sociology of success that is attuned to the real sources of resilience and flourishing in America.

What I'm proposing here, in other words, is a modest change in our stance toward our country and the social crisis it confronts. Not a social revolution or a political transformation, at least not directly. Just a greater awareness of how integrity, trust, confidence, belonging, and meaning are established in our lives—and so a greater care about some habits we have gotten into that tend to cut us off from them.

I'm asking you to consider the problems we face in the context of institutions, and to talk about them and act toward them in that context. To act through institutions a bit more, not just atop or against or around them. And, in acting through them, to strengthen and reform them: not just to trust our institutions but to make them more trustworthy.

Thinking and speaking just a little differently about how we live together can make a bigger difference than you might imagine. It can help us to see what we've been missing, to do what we've been neglecting, to say what we have only assumed or taken for granted. Small steps like those are what make great changes possible. They are constructive, and so they build upon each other and turn us all into builders.

That, in the end, is the character of the transformation we need. The demolition crews have for too long been allowed to define the spirit of this era in America. But where we're headed will be up to the builders and rebuilders. And that is what we each should seek to be.

ACKNOWLEDGMENTS

T HIS BOOK BEGAN AS A SERIES OF LECTURES, THE ANNUAL Charles E. Test Lectures, delivered at Princeton University in the spring of 2018. I am grateful to Princeton's department of politics and to the James Madison Program in American Ideals and Institutions for inviting me to deliver those lectures, and for the extraordinarily engaged and intelligent audiences that turned out for each one. Robert George, the founder and leader of the Madison Program, is a hero of mine and of countless other scholars of my generation. I'm grateful to him for more than I could list here, including his suggestion that the lectures might be expanded into a book.

The voices of two other teachers echo through these pages with particular force. One is Leon Kass, who has been for me a mentor and a model since I first had the good fortune to find myself in his classroom as a graduate student at the University of Chicago two decades ago. I am indebted to him in particular for the emphasis on forms that is at the heart of the argument of this book (and more generally for teaching me to paraphrase Aristotle, which is more or less my only marketable skill). My other teacher in these matters was the late Hugh Heclo, whose approach to the question of institutions decisively shaped my own—even where we disagree. His wisdom is sorely missed in these perplexing times.

Several friends and colleagues have gone above and beyond in helping me think through the themes of this book. Jon Ward has been a source of inspiration and encouragement from start to finish. His own examinations of the challenges of institutional decay and reformation—in his writing and in his podcast, *The Long Game*—have constituted some of the most important and creative journalistic work in Washington over the past several years. April Lawson was an invaluable sounding board for me from the very beginning of this work, and she devoted an enormous amount of time and effort to reading the manuscript at an early stage and providing wise comments and suggestions that proved very helpful.

Pete Wehner and David Brooks also read the lectures from which this book began and offered characteristically valuable insights and advice. Pete also read the final manuscript and gave me very helpful comments, as did Adam Keiper, Nicole Penn, Emily MacLean, Devorah Goldman, and Daniel Wiser. Along the way, I benefitted immensely from conversations about the themes of this book with Reihan Salam, Jonah Goldberg, Michael Gerson, Ben O'Dell, Ramesh Ponnuru, Ross Douthat, J. D. Vance, Jacob Reses, Jon Rauch, and Scott Winship.

I am also grateful to a number of magazine editors—particularly Rich Lowry of *National Review* and John Podhoretz of *Commentary*—who allowed me to work out some of the ideas in this book in their pages.

From 2007 until 2019, I was privileged to hang my hat at the Ethics and Public Policy Center in Washington, and much of my work on this book was done there, surrounded by wonderful colleagues and friends. Since 2009, I have also been lucky enough to serve as editor of *National Affairs* magazine, and my superb team there has made it a joy—my thanks to them all. Since the summer of 2019, I have made my professional home at the American Enterprise Institute, and I could hardly ask for greater good fortune than to find myself at America's foremost public-policy research institute and in the company of such extraordinary people. Neither this book nor my other work in recent years could have been possible without the generous support, encouragement, and wise guidance of Roger Hertog, for which I am deeply grateful.

At Basic Books, I have been fortunate to work with Lara Heimert and with Connor Guy—whose patient advice and sheer editing skill have improved this book far more than I am comfortable admitting to myself. Kelly Lenkevich, Elizabeth Dana, and Katie Lambright also offered vital improvements and help.

All of these friends, colleagues, advisors, and editors have improved the final product beyond measure. The many faults it still retains are my doing, and are in many cases even functions of my stubborn refusal to take great advice.

My greatest debt, however, is as always to my family. I am grateful to my parents for more than I could ever say. I am grateful to my children, Maya and Samuel, who have helped me learn what sheer joy feels like. But above all, I am grateful to, and grateful for, my wonderful wife, Cecelia. No one I have ever known embodies a commitment to do good in the world, grounded by a deep appreciation of the dignity of every single person, as fully as she does. She is amazing. I dedicate this book to her with love and gratitude, and with the sort of easy smile I never knew until I met her.

NOTES

INTRODUCTION

1. Robert Nisbet, *Twilight of Authority* (Indianapolis: Liberty Fund, 2000), xi.

2. Regarding my own work, I refer here in particular to my book *The Fractured Republic: Renewing America's Social Contract in the Age of Individualism* (New York: Basic Books, 2016). That book took up the question of the roots of our divisions in the liberalization of American life since the middle of the twentieth century. It was a study of the sources of the ethos of this moment in the evolution of our political culture, rather than a study of the forms and deformations of our social life; it focused on structural factors, whereas this book takes up the institutions of society. That book naturally intersects in some places with this one—each can deepen and explain the other some, since they are rooted in the same worldview. But this book is not an extension of that one, as it takes up a different set of questions from a different angle of approach. I will surrender to authorial vanity and refer the reader to that book once or twice in these pages, though only in the notes. But the reader will miss nothing here by having (shockingly!) neglected to read that book.

3. It is worth drawing attention to two particular ways in which I likely bring to the table some distinct limitations of the contemporary Right. The first is straightforward: as a conservative, I tend to be quick to defend the necessary preconditions for human flourishing, order, and freedom but to be slow to see the ways in which the status quo can be oppressive. Since I know this, I try to correct for it. But to see one's own deficiencies is not to overcome them, and I have no doubt—especially given the particular subject of this book—that I have not entirely surmounted that shortcoming here. Second, the intellectual world of the Right now absolutely overflows with political theorists and economists but desperately lacks sociologists and historians. By training, I'm a political theorist, and while I will try to avoid excessive abstraction and to draw upon the wisdom of sociologists, historians, and other social scientists and humanists, I'm sure that I cannot entirely overcome the dangerous professional tendency to treat practice as applied theory or otherwise to flatten or mistake the complicated and decidedly reciprocal relationship between the two.

4. Nisbet, *Twilight of Authority*, 259.

CHAPTER 1: THE MISSING LINKS

1. Data on social interactions, isolation, and loneliness are not simple to gather or interpret, and there are some significant disputes among analysts. Above all, the question of whether Americans are more lonely than usual today is contested. A good overview of that dispute—and source of data on reported numbers of friends, social activity, engagement, and isolation—is a 2018 report by the professional staff of the US Congress's Joint Economic Committee. The report, titled *All the Lonely Americans?*, argues persuasively that "loneliness" may not be the right term to describe the relevant trends, but it also takes note of troubling patterns in reported social activity, numbers of friends, time spent alone, and sense of engagement. Other key sources include the *2018 Cigna U.S. Loneliness Index: Survey of 20,000 Americans Examining Behaviors Driving Loneliness in the United States*, published by the health insurer Cigna, and Matthew Brashears, "Small Networks and High Isolation? A Reexamination of American Discussion Networks," *Social Networks* 33 (2011): 331–341.

2. For suicide deaths, see Centers for Disease Control and Prevention, *Morbidity and Mortality Weekly Report* 67, no. 22 (June 8, 2018). For "deaths of despair," see Anne Case and Angus Deaton, "Mortality and Morbidity in the 21st Century," *Brookings Papers on Economic Activity* (Spring 2017). For decline in overall life expectancy, see the CDC's data on trends in life expectancy at www.cdc.gov/nchs/fastats/life-expectancy.htm.

3. Holly Hedegaard, Arialdi M. Miniño, and Margaret Warner, *Drug Overdose Deaths in the United States, 1999–2017*, NCHS Data Brief (Hyattsville, MD: National Center for Health Statistics, 2018), www.cdc.gov/nchs/data/databriefs/db329-h.pdf.

4. The Great Recession formally ended at the end of the second quarter of 2009. For data on key trends across the income scale, see for instance the State of Working America Data Library at the Economic Policy Institute (www.epi.org/data/). These data certainly suggest slowed growth in the incomes of many working Americans, but they do not reveal a pattern that aligns with the pattern of social and cultural breakdown we have seen in any straightforward way. Economic pressures are clearly part of the story, but they do not explain the whole.

5. According to the US Justice Department's Uniform Crime Reporting Statistics, the nationwide violent-crime rate in 2017 was the lowest since 1970.

6. Steven Pinker, *Enlightenment Now: The Case for Reason, Science, Humanism, and Progress* (New York: Viking, 2018); Steven Pinker, "The Enlightenment Is Working," *Wall Street Journal*, February 10, 2018.

7. This view has long been identified with the communitarian Left (the work of Harvard's Michael Sandel offers some examples), but it has also expressed itself in recent years on the Right in a series of sharp critiques of the liberal tradition as a foundation for American life. Notable examples include Patrick Deneen's *Why Liberalism Failed* (New Haven, CT: Yale University Press, 2018), Yoram Hazony's *The Virtue of Nationalism* (New York: Basic Books, 2018), and numerous essays and articles, particularly from religious traditionalists.

8. These are entirely mainstream views among social conservatives and progressive liberals, respectively, articulated over decades in countless forms and arenas.

9. The new institutionalism might be traced as far back as the late 1970s and early 1980s, especially in sociology. But it did not become dominant until the 1990s and (particularly in my own field of political science) into the twenty-first century. The term "new institutionalism" is capacious enough to include a wide variety of different kinds of subfields and disciplinary insights, but I would argue that what is most important about it is that the idea of the institution has come to be an organizing principle for the work of these disciplines, so that their subfields and specializations (again, especially in sociology, but in some respects beyond it) have been understood as different ways to study and analyze institutions. This new approach to taking institutions seriously has flowered in ways that have made it not a return to the prior era of institutionalist social science but a real advance over it. That prior era ended in the middle decades of the twentieth century, when scholars with various kinds of critiques of a fundamentally institution-minded social science broke from that mainstream and eventually broke it altogether. Behavioralists, rational-choice theorists, and assorted post-modernists offered alternatives for understanding the sources and motives of political, social, and economic action and argued persuasively that the kind of comparative institutionalism that had dominated political science and sociology had grown too rigid and formulaic. But the social sciences could not remain divorced from the study of institutions for long. When those fields returned to institutions, they did so armed with some important insights from the work of these dissidents and critics. The new institutionalism, particularly in this century, has therefore been more sophisticated about motives, more alert to incentives and biases, more skeptical of formal restraints on power, and more sensitive to the significance of history and context in common action. As will be discussed, the definition of "institution" at the center of this transformation is often much more focused on rules than is the definition I will want to employ in this book, but the work of the new institutionalism is without question the foundation for my efforts here.

10. Hugh Heclo, *On Thinking Institutionally* (Oxford: Oxford University Press, 2008), 46–56. Heclo sought to categorize the definitions he reviewed as falling into five different schools of institutionalism (statist, social-systems, historical, rational-choice, and cognitive institutionalism). I do not think a similar catalog would be of use here, and in my view Heclo's definition

inclines too much in the direction of institutions as rules—a direction over-whelmingly preferred by economists, but one I ultimately consider much too narrow given the actual uses to which we put the term in our everyday language. Nonetheless, his review of modern definitions is enormously valuable and clarifying. My avoiding a full literature review here is by no means intended to disparage the institutionalism of the contemporary so-cial sciences, which I think has been very productive and in some respects very impressive. I have learned from that work, and will refer to it through-out, but there is little use in putting the reader through a torturous demon-stration of its breadth.

11. This definition is capacious in a particular way that requires a de-fense. To ease the way toward a manageable definition of the term, some scholars have sought to distinguish institutions from some of the functions they perform. Alasdair MacIntyre, a professor of philosophy at the Uni-versity of Notre Dame and one of the most important social theorists of our time, distinguishes "institution" from "practice," for instance. "Chess, physics and medicine are practices," he writes, while "chess clubs, labo-ratories and hospitals are institutions. . . . They are involved in acquiring money and other material goods; they are structured in terms of power and status, and they distribute money, power and status as rewards. Nor could they do otherwise if they are to sustain not only themselves, but also the practices of which they are the bearers" (Alasdair MacIntyre, *After Virtue* [Notre Dame, IN: University of Notre Dame Press, 1981], 194). This distinction allows MacIntyre to describe practices as essentially pristine and institutions as external sources of the corruption of practice. I would argue that what he calls practices are contained within institutions or are kinds of institutions. The difference is not semantic but substantive, because it sug-gests that, in instances of institutional corruption, institutions are not ex-ternal corroders but the thing being corrupted. What goes wrong is a loss of institutional integrity, in the form of a loss of focus on the institution's own purpose in favor of an external purpose foreign to it. This distinction and its implications will become clearer in the coming chapters.

Meanwhile, F. A. Hayek, especially in his *Counter-Revolution of Science* (In-dianapolis, IN: Liberty Fund, 1980), draws a distinction between "institution" and "formation"—essentially arguing that institutions are the result of in-tentional design, while formations arise through spontaneous, adaptive evolution from the bottom up. I think this distinction obscures more than it reveals and insists on too stark a distinction between design and evolution. In any case, I certainly mean to include in my definition of "institutions" what Hayek calls "formations," and it seems to me that an understanding of institutions as durable forms of associational life (as laid out at greater length in this chapter) would encompass both concepts as Hayek defines them.

12. Robert N. Bellah, Richard Madsen, William M. Sullivan, Ann Swidler, and Steven M. Tipton, in their brilliant book *The Good Society* (New York: Vintage, 1991), argue for defining an institution as "a pattern of expected actions" enforceable by law or norm. This is a strong version of the case for institutions as essentially functions of rules. But in ultimately defining an institution as a pattern of actions, it seems to me to leave out a range of institutions that are fundamentally conceptual or cognitive. I lean on the broader term "form" because it comes closer to capturing the immense breadth of what we expect institutions to be and do.

13. The example of form and matter as the shape and wax of a candle is itself Aristotle's (in *On the Soul*, 412b5–6), and my use of the concept of form here is more generally drawn from Aristotle's "hylomorphism," as articulated in *On the Soul*, the *Physics*, the *Metaphysics*, the *Categories*, and elsewhere.

14. This is another reason why it is a mistake to confound "institution" with "organization." There is a dubious thread in liberal thought that conceives of institutions in mechanistic terms—as machines with parts that act on the world—and views them as ways of moving people to behave in socially constructive ways, even if their intentions are purely selfish. James Madison nods in this direction when he notes, in a particularly Machiavellian passage of *Federalist* no. 51, that the American Constitution embodies a "policy of supplying, by opposite and rival interests, the defect of better motives" (*The Federalist Papers*, ed. R. B. Bernstein [New York: Arcturus, 2016], 319). I do not think this is what institutions do (and Madison elsewhere suggests he does not either). The conception of institutions I propose here points rather to a pre-liberal idea of formation—formation of the soul through habituation in virtue—in which institutions understood as social forms play a crucial role not as substitutes for personal formation but as means toward it.

15. A term like "social capital" is the epitome of what the essayist and social critic Helen Andrews has aptly called "bloodless moralism." It is a

way of describing what is obviously good and important in terms that seek through the paraphernalia of the social sciences to put some distance between us and the Jewish or Christian ideal of the good life that has shaped our civilization. Its employment is something of a concession to a mind-set that cannot acknowledge the truth of the teachings of our moral traditions unless they can be shown to also be of value in terms of the most crude, economistic, utilitarian sensibility. There is something ridiculous about such a way of speaking. And yet, despite itself, it also suggests an openness to traditional moral appeals even in the most self-consciously secular and technocratic precincts of our culture. Such openness among one's neighbors and fellow citizens should be looked at as an opportunity for persuasion and for finding common ground, and so should not be ridiculed even when it almost asks to be. We are all a little ridiculous when we evince our limitations without quite admitting them. Each of us does this in some way. And yet it is in these unacknowledged admissions that some of the most promising seeds of moral and intellectual progress may be found. I therefore use the term here, in the hope that it might be accessible to readers not otherwise inclined to think in more traditional terms of human flourishing and moral virtue, despite the term's plain limitations. (On bloodless moralism, see Helen Andrews, "Bloodless Moralism," *First Things*, February 2014.)

16. We live in a time that overflows with varied and interesting ways to spend social capital yet is desperately lacking in ways to amass it. In that fact is the key to a great many of our most important and complicated problems, and to the difficulties we face in understanding those problems.

17. Alexis de Tocqueville, *Democracy in America*, trans. Harvey C. Mansfield and Delba Winthrop (Chicago: University of Chicago Press, 2000), 404.

18. On this point, see also Samuel Huntington, *American Politics: The Promise of Disharmony* (Cambridge, MA: Belknap Press, 1981).

CHAPTER 2: FROM MOLDS TO PLATFORMS

1. Lower confidence in the military in the 1970s was of course very likely a function of the controversial nature of the Vietnam War, but it persisted in Gallup's data until the end of the 1980s. All of Gallup's Confidence in Institutions data, as well as ongoing surveys regarding particular

institutions, are available online at https://news.gallup.com/poll/1597 /confidence-institutions.aspx. The Pew Research Center, which conducts detailed trend studies in public opinion, offers additional support for the same impression of public attitudes. Although Pew's data do not go as far back as Gallup's, they suggest a sharpening of the decline in public confidence in key institutions in this century. They also show that the pattern is evident throughout the West, not just in the United States. Pew's research on trust in institutions is collected at www.pewresearch.org/topics /trust-in-government/.

2. Basic incompetence may seem like a strange fit for this list, as it does not necessarily denote corruption or abuse. But opinion research has long shown that, particularly with respect to government institutions, poor performance is connected in the public mind with corruption, and leads by the same path to loss of trust. See especially Kenneth Newton and Pippa Norris, "Confidence in Public Institutions: Faith, Culture or Performance?" (paper for presentation at the Annual Meeting of the American Political Science Association, Atlanta, GA, September 1–5, 1999), https://sites.hks .harvard.edu/fs/pnorris/Acrobat/NEWTON.PDF.

3. In his 1962 book *The Image*, the great historian Daniel J. Boorstin famously defined the celebrity as "a person known for being well known." That definition suggests the nature of the connection between platform institutions and the culture of celebrity. Celebrity is a measure of generic well-knownness of a sort that can be achieved on a generic platform. It also avoids imposing any standard on us, since the celebrity is not generally known for embodying any particular virtue that we might be tempted to emulate. As Boorstin put it, "Celebrities are made by the people. The hero stood for outside standards. The celebrity is a tautology. We still try to make our celebrities stand in for the heroes we no longer have, or for those who have been pushed out of our view. We forget celebrities are known primarily for their well-knownness. And we imitate them as if they were cast in the mold of greatness. Yet the celebrity is usually nothing greater than a more-publicized version of us. In imitating him, in trying to dress like him, talk like him, look like him, think like him we are simply imitating ourselves. By imitating a tautology, we ourselves become a tautology: standing for what we stand for, reaching to become more emphatically what we already are. When we praise our famous

men we pretend to look out the window of history. We do not like to confess that we are looking into a mirror. We look for models, and we see our own image." Daniel J. Boorstin, *The Image* (New York: Penguin Random House, 1962), 74.

4. This transformation of the American ethos, away from the cohesion of the middle of the twentieth century, was the subject of my 2016 book *The Fractured Republic*. The trends described here very briefly are laid out at much greater length there.

5. On this front, too, Boorstin's *The Image* stands as an unrivaled work of prophecy. Still in print, it is as timely as ever, and offers some extraordinary premonitions of the direction American social life has taken.

6. The political scientist Hugh Heclo, who was a great scholar of these subjects, nicely summarized the way this works: "From inside an institutional worldview," he wrote, "when approaching a major choice the question is not, 'How can I get what I want?' It is the duty-laden question that asks, 'What expectations and conduct are appropriate to my position and the choices I might make?'" Heclo, *Thinking Institutionally*, 102.

CHAPTER 3: WE THE PEOPLE

1. Hans Kohn, *American Nationalism* (New York: Macmillan, 1957), 8. The sheer continuity of our system of government surely has had a lot to do with this. The Capitol Building, in Washington, DC, opened in 1800 to house the same institution—the US Congress—it still houses today. In the course of that same 220-year period, the arrangement of powers in even the exceptionally steady British regime has gone through dramatic transformations unlike anything we have witnessed here, and most other relatively stable societies (like the nations of western Europe, Russia, China, Japan, and countless others) have gone through several fundamental changes of regime through conquest, revolution, or political upheaval. The French have lived under five republics and a handful of other forms of government in that time. We Americans sometimes still think of ourselves as a young nation, but our political institutions are among the most established in the world.

2. *Federalist*, 62, 65.

3. Josh Kraushaar, "Alexandria Ocasio-Cortez Testing the Limits of Political Celebrity," *National Journal*, February 17, 2019.

4. Alexis Levinson, "This Florida Congressman Is Trump's Ultimate Defender and Doesn't Care if He's Notorious," *Buzzfeed*, February 8, 2018.

5. *Federalist*, 319.

6. In 1976, the writer and editor Irving Kristol took to the pages of the *New York Times* to make this point:

> Take, for instance, the so-called "sunshine" laws which are being passed at every level of government, and against which no public figure seems bold enough to protest. They require that practically all meetings of all official bodies be open to public view. This sounds good, but in actuality it is utterly absurd. It's no way to run anything, whether it be a school board, a university department, a trade union or a government agency. It penalizes candor and compromise and rewards aggressive "grandstanding." Does anyone really believe that the Ford Motor Company and the United Automobile Workers could have reached an agreement if their negotiations were transmitted live on television? Or even if minutes of the meetings were kept? Similarly, the only reason Congress can function is because the committee system provides private (i.e., "secret") occasions for negotiation that are distinct from the public forum where opinions are sharply expressed and debated.

Irving Kristol, "Post-Watergate Morality: Too Good for Our Good?," *New York Times Magazine*, November 14, 1976, 50.

7. There is enormous tension between these different models of reforming Congress, which speaks to a tension in our understanding of the nature and purpose of our political institutions. Reforms that strengthen party organization in Congress and reforms that strengthen its institutional assertiveness are almost bound to point in opposite directions, because party cohesion crosses institutional lines and encourages the subservience of Congress to an executive of the same party, or else the harnessing of Congress in opposition to the executive of the opposite party. Neither of these amounts to a reinforcement of the institutional position of the Congress. Such reinforcement would need to encourage cross-party coalitions and would cut against the grain of contemporary partisanship more generally. This tension is too often ignored in many contemporary discussions of congressional reform, which quickly devolve into attacks against the

filibuster and calls for more parliamentary government. In a brilliant 2015 paper entitled *Two Pathways for Congressional Reform*, political scientist Daniel Stid lays out these two paths, which he dubs Wilsonian and Madisonian reform—the former pushing in the direction of parliamentary government and a presidential model of governance and the latter pointing toward the separation of powers with Congress in the driver's seat. The Madisonian approach strikes me as by far the better suited to the challenges we face now, but it is almost absent from the discussion of congressional reform in both political science and political journalism. Daniel Stid, *Two Pathways for Congressional Reform* (Menlo Park, CA: William and Flora Hewlett Foundation, 2015), https://hewlett.org/wp-content/uploads/2018/01/Two-Pathways-for-Congressional-Reform_March-2015.pdf.

8. On this subject, the work of the great American historian Douglass Adair, particularly the essays gathered in his 1971 collection *Fame and the Founding Fathers* (Indianapolis, IN: Liberty Fund, 1998), remains second to none.

9. Henry J. Gomez, "Trump Supporters Boo a CNN Reporter, Then Ask Him for Selfies," *Buzzfeed*, June 25, 2018.

10. Consider how the Supreme Court majority began its landmark opinion in a 2015 case involving same-sex marriage, for instance: "Marriage responds to the universal fear that a lonely person might call out only to find no one there. It offers the hope of companionship and understanding and assurance that while both still live there will be someone to care for the other." It's a lovely sentiment, whatever your view about the subject matter. But it is not jurisprudence. And it isn't quite rooted in some alternative theory about the proper constitutional role of the judge, either. So, what is it? In too many cases now, for too many judges, it is a kind of performance, a display of virtue for the sake of an audience. Obergefell v. Hodges, 135 S. Ct. 2584 (2015).

11. Both because of the character of our separation of powers (in the states and at the federal level) and because of the nature of the electoral rules that govern our legislative elections, the American system strongly discourages fragmentation into smaller parties like those seen in systems that involve more proportional representation.

12. E. E. Schattschneider, *Party Government* (New York: Rinehart & Company, 1942), 60.

13. See, for instance, Elaine C. Kamarck, *Re-inserting Peer Review in the American Presidential Nomination Process* (Washington, DC: Brookings Institution, 2017).

14. See, for instance, Christopher A. Bail et al., "Exposure to Opposing Views on Social Media Can Increase Political Polarization," *Proceedings of the National Academy of Sciences*, September 11, 2018.

CHAPTER 4: PROFESSIONAL HELP

1. The sociology of the professions is a long-established field, but it has been reenergized in recent years and begun to take a prominent place within the new institutionalism in sociology. For a good overview of the state of the field, see Daniel Muzio, David M. Brock, and Roy Suddaby, "Professions and Institutional Change: Towards an Institutionalist Sociology of the Professions," *Journal of Management Studies* 50, no. 5 (July 2013): 699–721.

2. Donald J. Trump (@realDonaldTrump), "The Fake News Media has never been so wrong or so dirty. Purposely incorrect stories and phony sources to meet their agenda of hate. Sad!," Twitter, https://twitter.com/realdonaldtrump/status/874576057579565056.

3. The commission's members—along with Hutchins they were Zechariah Chafee, John M. Clark, John Dickinson, William E. Hocking, Harold Lasswell, Archibald MacLeish, Charles Merriam, Reinhold Niebuhr, Robert Redfield, Beardsley Ruml, Arthur Schlesinger, and George N. Shuster—were scholars and intellectuals, but none were journalists or otherwise much involved in the work of the press. This contributed to what both critics and defenders acknowledged was an outsider's view of American journalism in the commission's work, focused particularly on the relationship of journalism to the larger society.

4. Commission on Freedom of the Press, *A Free and Responsible Press* (Chicago: University of Chicago Press, 1947), 3.

5. Commission on Freedom of the Press, *Free and Responsible*, 5.

6. Although the essay was originally anonymous, there is no dispute about Franklin's authorship. An authoritative text, used here for all citations, can be found in Albert Henry Smyth, ed., *The Writings of Benjamin Franklin* (New York: Macmillan Co., 1905), 10:36–40. For an exceptionally

valuable analysis of Franklin's essay, see Arthur Milikh, "Franklin and the Free Press," *National Affairs*, Spring 2017, 129–141.

7. Smyth, *Writings of Benjamin Franklin*, 10:38.

8. Smyth, *Writings of Benjamin Franklin*, 10:40.

9. Franklin was himself a prominent printer and publisher, and at several points in his career made forthright arguments in defense of the freedom of the press as essential to the preservation of liberty and good government. A useful source on this front is Lorraine Smith Pangle, *The Political Philosophy of Benjamin Franklin* (Baltimore: Johns Hopkins University Press, 2007).

10. For a fuller history of these trends, understood in these terms, see my book *The Fractured Republic*.

11. One famous illustration of the character of this self-confidence is the fact that the Columbia School of Journalism confers a master of *science* degree in journalism.

12. For Gallup's historical figures, see Art Swift, "Americans' Trust in Mass Media Sinks to New Low," Gallup, September 14, 2016, www.gallup .com/poll/195542/americans-trust-mass-media-sinks-new-low.aspx.

13. Joe Pompeo, "'Journalism Is Not about Creating Safe Spaces': Inside the Woke Civil War at the *New York Times*," *Vanity Fair*, April 3, 2018.

14. On the evolution of the legal profession, see, for instance, Anthony T. Kronman, *The Lost Lawyer: Failing Ideals of the Legal Profession* (Cambridge, MA: Belknap Press, 1993).

CHAPTER 5: CAMPUS CULTURES

1. On Harvard in particular, see, for instance, Michael G. Hall, *The Last American Puritan: The Life of Increase Mather* (Middletown, CT: Wesleyan University Press, 1992), 279–289. On the history of American higher education, two excellent sources are Frederick Rudolph's *The American College and University: A History* (1962, repr. Athens: University of Georgia Press, 1990) and John R. Thelin's *A History of American Higher Education* (Baltimore: Johns Hopkins University Press, 2004).

2. Robert A. Nisbet, *The Degradation of the Academic Dogma* (New York: Transaction Publishers, 1997), 8.

3. "Undergraduate Degree Fields," National Center for Education Statistics, last updated March 2018.

4. As Robert Nisbet puts it, "The relation between the university and the professions has always been a close one. No greater fallacy concerning the university is imaginable than that of supposing it to be, historically, a mere haven for the liberal arts and for individuals of contemplative mind or of monastic inclination alone. From the founding of the university in Bologna and Paris around the professional areas of theology, law, and medicine down to the American university that is today so rich in professional schools, covering a large number of social needs, there is a straight line" (Nisbet, *Academic Dogma*, 128). Alexis de Tocqueville noted that this was particularly evident in universities in the United States, where the heavy emphasis on professional and scientific training was striking (Tocqueville, *Democracy in America*, 451).

5. Hastings Rashdall, *The Universities of Europe in the Middle Ages*, vol. 2, part 2, *English Universities, Student Life* (Cambridge: Cambridge University Press, 2010), ch. 14. A useful source on the history of American campus activism is Christopher J. Broadhurst, "Campus Activism in the 21st Century: A Historical Framing," *New Directions for Higher Education*, no. 167 (Fall 2014).

6. Smith writes, "American sociology as a collective enterprise is at heart committed to the visionary project of realizing the emancipation, equality, and moral affirmation of all human beings as autonomous, self-directing, individual agents (who should be) out to live their lives as they personally so desire, by constructing their own favored identities, entering and exiting relationships as they choose, and equally enjoying the gratification of experimental, material, and bodily pleasures." Christian Smith, *The Sacred Project of American Sociology* (Oxford: Oxford University Press, 2014), 8.

7. The first known occurrence of the term "liberal arts" appears to be in Cicero's *De Inventione*, in the first century BC, though his use of it suggests he did not invent the term.

8. Leo Strauss, "What Is Liberal Education?," in *An Introduction to Political Philosophy: Ten Essays by Leo Strauss*, ed. Hilail Gildin (Detroit: Wayne State University Press, 1989), 314. Although liberal education is not conservative in a political sense, considering it in light of its relation to the culture of moral activism on most campuses suggests an implicit kinship

with a broadly conservative outlook on the nature of social change. One way to conceive of the Left and the Right in our politics, very broadly understood, is that each wants to direct society's attention toward some things otherwise taken for granted: conservatives want us to see the good things we take for granted (like our traditions and the inherited cultural achievements that we did not build but should be grateful for and work to preserve), while progressives want us to see the bad things we take for granted (like the marginalization of some in our society and the injustices we fail to notice). The culture of social activism on campus is very much about raising consciousness about injustices we take for granted, and so showing us what we should know to be a good society, while the culture of liberal education seeks to raise consciousness about the wonderful cultural inheritances we take for granted, and so showing us what we should know to sustain our civilizational treasures. Both, at their best, are educative— they are about revealing things we do not see or know. Neither needs to be attached to the policy agenda of any political faction or party. But the two do bear at times a relation to the general dispositions of the Left and Right more broadly.

9. The culture of natural science was a far more powerful influence on the larger academic culture in the middle of the twentieth century than it is today, however, and it is no longer plausible to speak (as C. P. Snow famously did in mid-century Britain) of our intellectual life as divided into a culture of scientists and a culture of humanists. The progressive ideal of natural science as offering society a path to material and moral advancement, which would have surely been described as a powerful ethos of academic life throughout much of the last century, was sharply diminished by its clashes with various kinds of postmodern challengers, so that its sociopolitical character has largely been subsumed by a broader culture of moral activism and its earnest search after the reality of nature wherever it may lead is now probably better understood as an element of the culture of liberal education. These two facets of that older scientific ethos are sometimes in tension themselves, and will probably be in such tension more often in the coming years. And the result of that tension will probably be that scientific research comes to seem more like a facet of professional development than of either of the other cultures I've described, let alone a strong, independent cultural force. The culture of scientific research still matters,

of course, but today it is simply not as coherent, powerful, and distinct a force in the larger life of the academy as it was in recent generations.

10. As Shields further notes, "This problem is especially acute on the campuses of elite liberal-arts colleges. According to a recent study on faculty party affiliation by the National Association of Scholars, the ratio of Democrats to Republicans at Williams College is 132:1; at Swarthmore it is 120:1; and at Bryn Mawr it is 72:0. At many of America's best research universities, the ratios are only moderately better." Jon A. Shields, "The Disappearing Conservative Professor," *National Affairs*, Fall 2018, 139.

11. Arnold Kling, *The Three Languages of Politics: Talking Across Political Divides* (Washington, DC: Cato Institute, 2017).

12. Harvey Mansfield, "The State of Harvard," *Public Interest*, Fall 1990, 118.

13. There is an entire book to be written about the nature and sources of this confusion of extreme egalitarianism with nihilism. Among the very few instances of its being noticed and debated has been a heated argument among different strands of the school of political philosophy rooted in the work of Leo Strauss and his students. Debates about American politics among Straussians of different flavors have often involved disputes about whether the Left is best understood as radically egalitarian (as thinkers like Edmund Burke and Alexis de Tocqueville tended to see it), and therefore is best answered by a kind of classical political moderation, or whether it is best understood through more Germanic categories like nihilism and historicism, and therefore best answered by recourse to a classically rationalist politics of natural right. The first understanding, which is more Anglo-American and has its deepest roots in both the era and the transatlantic cultural milieu of the American founding, strikes me as more persuasive than the second, which is more German and postmodern, and is therefore less obviously at home in our political tradition. But surely both have something of the truth.

14. Alan Jacobs, "Wokeness and Myth on Campus," *New Atlantis*, Summer/Fall 2017, 33–44.

15. My own experiences on numerous campuses in recent years offer ample evidence as well that activist progressives in the academy are blissfully unaware of how aggressive and threatening they can seem to conservatives. A visit to an Ivy League law school in 2016 left a particular

impression on me. I had been invited to speak to students and faculty about religious liberty, and at dinner with a small group afterward it became apparent to me that my claims that many religious traditionalists felt threatened by attempts to punish believers for opposing same-sex marriage were unfamiliar news to everyone around the table. They were aware of the basic facts of some of the incidents I mentioned, but had no sense whatsoever that these might have led to widespread concern. They were not cynical about or even dismissive of these concerns. They simply had no idea they existed.

16. April Lawson, "Heterodoxy to the Rescue," *Comment*, Spring 2018, 35–42.

17. Seymour Martin Lipset, "The Activists: A Profile," *Public Interest*, Fall 1968, 47.

CHAPTER 6: THE INFORMALITY MACHINE

1. I owe this distinction between substitute and supplement to Joshua Mitchell, who laid it out to me in conversation but has since articulated it most fully in his excellent essay "When Supplements Become Substitutes," in the Autumn 2018 issue of *City Journal*.

2. Mark Zuckerberg, "Building Global Community," Facebook, February 16, 2017, www.facebook.com/notes/mark-zuckerberg/building-global -community/10103508221158471/. (Throughout this chapter, and throughout the book, I treat "social media" as a singular rather than a plural term. This is in line with how the term is increasingly used and with recent dictionary usages, though I recognize there are arguments for attaching it to plural terms, since media is the plural of medium.)

3. Max Read, "Does Even Mark Zuckerberg Know What Facebook Is?," *New York Magazine*, October 2, 2017.

4. In his (very) short story "A Radically Condensed History of Postindustrial Life," David Foster Wallace perfectly captures this social dynamic of online life: "When they were introduced, he made a witticism, hoping to be liked. She laughed extremely hard, hoping to be liked. Then each drove home alone, staring straight ahead, with the very same twist to their faces." David Foster Wallace, *Brief Interviews with Hideous Men* (New York: Little, Brown & Co., 1999), 1.

5. Jane Jacobs, *The Death and Life of Great American Cities* (New York: Random House, 1961). See particularly chapters 11 and 12.

6. Adam Mosseri, "Building a Better News Feed for You," Facebook (press release), https://newsroom.fb.com/news/2016/06/building-a-better-news-feed-for-you/.

7. Stephen Marche, "The Crisis of Intimacy in the Age of Digital Connectivity," *Los Angeles Review of Books*, October 15, 2018.

8. On the political implications of social media and the internet, no one has argued more persuasively than Martin Gurri. See especially his fantastic book *The Revolt of the Public: And the Crisis of Authority in the New Millennium* (San Francisco: Stripe Press, 2018).

9. Boorstin, *The Image*, 74.

10. This point is well argued in Glenn Harlan Reynolds, "Social Media Threat: People Learned to Survive Disease, We Can Handle Twitter," *USA Today*, November 20, 2017.

CHAPTER 7: CLOSE TO HOME

1. There is much more to be said about the state of family, church, and community in America than could be taken up in this short span. Our focus here will therefore be on the transformation of the institutional character of these essential foundries of the human being and the citizen, and on the transformation of our expectations of them as institutions. A further reason to constrain this discussion to these themes is that the state of family, religion, and community as intermediate institutions in our society was a core subject of a prior book of mine, *The Fractured Republic*. What follows here extends, without repeating, the argument of that book's later chapters.

2. The Pew Research Center provides a constantly updated and accessible set of data points on family formation and family structure at www.pewresearch.org/topics/household-and-family-structure/.

3. Gallup's polling on trends in religious attendance, trust in religious institutions, and the role of religion in American life provides a helpful trove of data on opinion trends. It can be found at https://news.gallup.com/poll/1690/religion.aspx.

4. Dividing the American population by religious affiliation is a notoriously complicated undertaking, since it requires grouping and distinguishing denominations and also determining what level of affiliation or practice ought to count in designating a given individual as a member of a certain group. I make no claim to any methodological innovation on this front and merely followed the most commonly cited measures, in this case as used by the Pew Research Center's Religious Landscape Study. In its most recent iteration, the study found that just over 25 percent of Americans were Evangelical Protestants, while roughly 21 percent were Catholics (though the latter number is likely an underestimate because of the difficulty of counting immigrant populations, which tend to be disproportionally Catholic). For a discussion of both the methodology and findings of this study as well as the complete results, see "Religious Landscape Study," Pew Research Center, www.pewforum.org /religious-landscape-study/.

5. Statistics regarding the abuse of children by various kinds of caregivers are obviously contested and hard to come by, but the available academic literature on the subject suggests Catholic priests do not stand out as abusers in relation to other adults in youth-serving organizations. For a useful overview, see for instance Anne Shattuck et al., "Children Exposed to Abuse in Youth-Serving Organizations: Results from National Sample Surveys," *JAMA Pediatrics* 170, no. 2 (February 2016).

6. Needless to say, these are hardly the only serious downsides to strong institutions. A number of others will be taken up in the next chapter.

7. On the percentage of Evangelicals who voted for Trump, see the *New York Times* archive of 2016 exit polling at Jon Huang et al., "Election 2016: Exit Polls," *New York Times*, www.nytimes.com/interactive/2016/11 /08/us/politics/election-exit-polls.html. On views regarding the dignity of the presidency, see *PRRI 2018 American Values Survey* (Washington, DC: PRRI, 2018), www.prri.org/wp-content/uploads/2018/10/AVS-2018-Topline -COMBINED.pdf; I cite results for white Catholics and Protestants to avoid the intense racial divide over Trump. On immoral personal behavior, see, for instance, William Saletan, "Trump's Christian Apologists Are Unchristian," *Slate*, November 25, 2018, https://slate.com/news-and-politics/2018 /11/trumps-christian-apologists-are-unchristian.html. The underlying surveys

cited here (and by Saletan) are Daniel Cox and Robert P. Jones, "Financial Misconduct Worse Than Sexual Misconduct for Public Officials," PRRI, June 22, 2011, www.prri.org/research/more-americans-say-financial-misconduct -by-elected-officials-is-a-very-serious-moral-problem-than-say-sexual -misconduct/, and "Backing Trump, White Evangelicals Flip Flop on Importance of Candidate Character: PRRI/Brookings Survey," PRRI, October 19, 2016, www.prri.org/research/prri-brookings-oct-19-poll-politics-election -clinton-double-digit-lead-trump/.

8. Marc Thiessen, "Why Conservative Christians Stick with Trump," *Washington Post*, March 23, 2018.

9. On Jerry Falwell Jr., see Sarah Rodriguez, "Falwell Speaks," *Liberty Champion*, March 8, 2016. On David Jeremiah, see Michael Gerson, "The Last Temptation," *Atlantic*, April 2018.

10. Alan Jacobs, "When Character No Longer Counts," *National Affairs*, Spring 2017.

11. Andy Crouch, "It's Time to Reckon with Celebrity Power," *Gospel Coalition*, March 24, 2018.

12. See, for instance, "A Rule of Life for Redemptive Entrepreneurs," Praxis, https://rule.praxislabs.org/.

13. These various efforts at rules include, for instance, Justin Whitmel Earley, "The Common Rule," www.thecommonrule.org/; "Every Moment Holy: New Liturgies for Daily Life," www.everymomentholy.com/; and "A Way Forward: Six Practices of the Church," http://sixpractices .qideas.org/.

14. The term "great awokening" appears to have originated with the journalist Andrew Sullivan. See Andrew Sullivan, "America's New Religions," *New York*, December 7, 2018.

15. José Ortega y Gasset, *The Revolt of the Masses* (New York: W. W. Norton, 2014), ch. 14. This sentiment had been expressed, if less concisely, by Max Weber, who was central to the development of key concepts in sociology well before Ortega y Gasset. I cite him here as a particularly valuable formulation of this idea, but not to suggest that he was the source of the insight as applied by sociologists and by communitarians in other disciplines.

16. Robert Nisbet, *The Quest for Community* (Wilmington, DE: Intercollegiate Studies Institute, 2014), 47.

17. Mike Allen, "Fast-Growing Global Trend: Pop-Up Protests," *Axios*, July 1, 2018, www.axios.com/donald-trump-protests-immigration-march -womens-rights-gun-control-ba50f45d-0dad-4abd-950f-c3c7283d93dd.html.

CHAPTER 8: THE CASE FOR COMMITMENT

1. Such institutions can still perform essential functions, and can even inspire a kind of loyalty. But as Max Weber understood, there is a big difference between loyalty to an office or machine and loyalty to a shared ideal and a group of people you feel part of. In this respect, the institutional might appear to be the opposite of the personal or the authentic. And in circumstances of excess rigidity, liberation can mean relief from the dominance of institutions. See particularly Max Weber, *Economy and Society: An Outline of Interpretive Sociology* (New York: Bedminster Press, 1968), 956–958.

2. In fact, proposals for recovering our lost solidarity and social capital often end up gesturing toward mass mobilization as the only way to really address the social crisis we confront. The search for historical analogies, for times when such problems have been well met, ends up with unnerving frequency reaching for examples of war footing or responses to extreme national crises. And so the friends of solidarity and cohesion risk yearning for a unifying calamity or sounding like nostalgics for terrible crises. At the very least, they often call for what William James famously termed "the moral equivalent of war." This is itself a cautionary downside of the case for institutionalism. To yearn for mass mobilization is implicitly to hope for suffering and tragedy, and no one should hope for those for our country. We should seek for ways to strengthen our institutions that do not require such dark catalysts.

3. See Heclo, *Thinking Institutionally*, 102.

4. Yoni Appelbaum, "Americans Aren't Practicing Democracy Anymore," *Atlantic*, October 2018.

5. Mary Douglas, *How Institutions Think* (Syracuse, NY: Syracuse University Press, 1986), 45.

6. This point is nowhere better articulated than in *Federalist* no. 1, in which Alexander Hamilton sets the scene for the debate over ratification of

the Constitution by offering an extraordinarily sophisticated guide to the social psychology of heated political disagreements.

7. Such a standard of judgment—even if pursued but never attained—is essential to any effort of moral improvement. As Abraham Lincoln said regarding the American commitment to equality, it offers "a standard maxim for free society, which should be familiar to all, and revered by all; constantly looked to, constantly labored for, and even though never perfectly attained, constantly approximated, and thereby constantly spreading and deepening its influence, and augmenting the happiness and value of life to all people of all colors everywhere." Abraham Lincoln, "Speech on the Dred Scott Decision," June 26, 1857.

8. In a eulogy for his great hero Henry Clay in 1852, Abraham Lincoln noted of Clay that "he loved his country partly because it was his own country, but mostly because it was a free country." Many of us live out our idealism this way. Abraham Lincoln, "Eulogy on Henry Clay," July 6, 1852, www.abrahamlincolnonline.org/lincoln/speeches/clay.htm.

9. There is a strand of the republican tradition, reaching back to Machiavelli through James Madison in certain moods, that suggests that our institutions actually act as substitutes for the kind of virtues that might be formed through experiences like these. But the countervailing tradition, reaching back to Aristotle through Adam Smith at his best, which sees our institutions as forming us to practice the virtues rather than saving us the trouble of doing so, is far more persuasive and plausible.

CHAPTER 9: BEYOND MERITOCRACY

1. Irving Kristol, "When Virtue Loses All Her Loveliness," *Public Interest*, Fall 1970, 9, 12.

2. In referring to these "secular moralisms," I have in mind for instance the appeal of Jordan Peterson, who has built a massive following by effectively telling young men to take their responsibilities more seriously.

3. Michael Young, *The Rise of the Meritocracy* (New York: Transaction Publishers, 2011), 11.

4. William Deresiewicz, *Excellent Sheep: The Miseducation of the American Elite and the Way to a Meaningful Life* (New York: Free Press, 2014), 205.

5. The nature of the criteria of merit at the heart of our meritocracy further contributes to this tendency. They are intellectual criteria, and so put forward a sterile, technocratic idea of power that tends to persuade today's elites that they have what it takes to rule. As Max Weber understood a century ago,

> Bureaucratic administration means fundamentally the exercise of control on the basis of knowledge. This is the feature of it which makes it specifically rational. This consists on the one hand in technical knowledge which, by itself, is sufficient to ensure it a position of extraordinary power. But in addition to this, bureaucratic organizations, or the holders of power who make use of them, have the tendency to increase their power still further by the knowledge growing out of experience in the service. For they acquire through the conduct of office a special knowledge of facts and have available a store of documentary material peculiar to themselves.

Max Weber, *The Theory of Social and Economic Organization*, trans. A. M. Henderson and Talcott Parsons (New York: The Free Press, 1947), 339.

6. Helen Andrews, "The New Ruling Class," *Hedgehog Review*, Summer 2016.

7. This is the opening line of Rousseau's *The Social Contract*. See *Rousseau: The Social Contract and Other Late Political Writings*, trans. Victor Gourevitch (Cambridge: Cambridge University Press, 2018), 351.

8. The form of the argument laid out in these pages is a function of my own worldview, and so it is a conservative idea, in the broadest conceptual sense. That is not to say that it is a case against the Left, or that it ought to be obnoxious to progressives, but its roots are in the Right's conception of the nature of society. It is not an all-purpose argument for strong institutions rooted in some measure of their practical utility alone. It is, rather, one implication of a moral vision grounded in a particular understanding of the human person, which sees each and every person as a fallen and imperfect creature, prone to excess and to sin, and ever in need of self-restraint and moral formation—and so of institutions

capable of providing such formation. It is no exaggeration to say that, for me, the inquiry pursued in this book began in contemplation of a peculiar and profound expression of Edmund Burke's: "Every sort of moral, every sort of civil, every sort of politic institution, aiding the rational and natural ties that connect the human understanding and affections to the divine, are not more than necessary, in order to build up that wonderful structure, Man—whose prerogative it is, to be in a great degree a creature of his own making, and who, when made as he ought to be made, is destined to hold no trivial place in the creation." Edmund Burke, *Revolutionary Writings*, ed. Iain Hampsher-Monk (Cambridge: Cambridge University Press, 2014), 96.

INDEX

MOSHE ZUSMAN

YUVAL LEVIN is director of social, cultural, and constitutional studies at the American Enterprise Institute and the editor of *National Affairs*. A former member of the White House domestic policy staff under George W. Bush, he has written for the *New York Times*, *Washington Post*, and *Wall Street Journal*, among many other publications. His previous books include *The Fractured Republic* and *The Great Debate*. He lives in Maryland.